QUANTUM VIBES

WELBECK
BALANCE

About the Author

Suzanne is a thought leader in the field of personal development, energetics, manifesting and leadership.

As a seasoned speaker who has taken the mic on NBC, The CW, Fox News and the TEDx stage, Suzanne Adams reaches across the globe to share her message of enlightenment, inspiration and transformation.

For more about Suzanne, go to www.suzanneadamsinc.com or follow her on social media @suzanneadamsinc.

QUANTUM VIBES

7 Tools to Raise Your Energy, Harness Your Power
and Manifest a Life That Will Blow Your Mind

by Suzanne Adams

WELBECK
BALANCE

Published in 2022 by Welbeck Balance
An imprint of Welbeck Trigger Ltd
Part of Welbeck Publishing Group
Based in London and Sydney
www.welbeckpublishing.com

A CIP catalogue record for this book is available from the British Library.

ISBN
Trade Paperback – 978-1-80129-120-0

Typeset by Lapiz Digital Services
Printed in Great Britain by CPI Group (UK) Ltd, Croydon CR0 4YY

10 9 8 7 6 5 4 3 2 1

MIX
Paper from
responsible sources
FSC® C171272

Note/Disclaimer
Welbeck Balance encourages diversity and different viewpoints.
However, all views, thoughts, and opinions expressed in this book are the
author's own and are not necessarily representative of Welbeck Publishing Group as
an organization. All material in this book is set out in good faith for general guidance;
Welbeck Publishing Group makes no representations or warranties of any kind, express or
implied, with respect to the accuracy, completeness, suitability or currency of the contents
of this book, and specifically disclaims, to the extent permitted by law, any implied
warranties of merchantability or fitness for a particular purpose and any injury, illness,
damage, death, liability or loss incurred, directly or indirectly from the use or application
of any of the information contained in this book. This book is not intended to replace
expert medical or psychiatric advice. It is intended for informational purposes only and
for your own personal use and guidance. It is not intended to diagnose, treat or
act as a substitute for professional medical advice. The author and the publisher
are not medical practitioners nor counsellors, and professional advice should be
sought before embarking on any health-related programme.

This book is truly a piece of my heart and soul and is dedicated to every brave human that is walking this path of evolution, growth, happiness and fulfillment right beside me!

Contents

Introduction

"If you change the way you look at things, the things you look at change."

Wayne Dyer

In religion we call it spirit. In science we call it energy. In the streets we call it vibes. In *Quantum Vibes* all I'm saying is to trust it – and get ready to create it from your heart and soul in such a powerful way it'll blow your mind.

Why do you need this book now? Because we're living in a time when we have the choice and opportunity to see things through a different lens. We can't control what has happened to us or around us, but we *can* control the way we show up in the world and how we choose to respond. *Quantum Vibes* provides the tools we need to answer the new, bigger and bolder callings we're all feeling.

The key to moving forward in this era of chaos and unpredictability is to understand – and use – your inner strength. To see yourself as an agent of change. Your thoughts and vibrations can not only help you manifest your dreams and desires but also uplift others and rally the planet toward making it a better place.

You already have this capacity – trust me, you do. And yet, you may be feeling overwhelmed by the upheaval around you. You might be feeling out of tune with yourself as well as buffeted by the mega forces at work. But at the same time, we can also be part of one of the largest mass awakenings. *Quantum Vibes* will give you the blueprint you need to help you use this momentum to strengthen your personal energy or life vibration. Doing so will empower you to connect to something divine, beyond you. Let me say it again: finding and honing a potent inner reality will enable you to manifest circumstances and desires that will light you up from the inside out – and from head to toe!

If you're anything like me, you want confidence. Joy. Connection. Passion. Purpose. *Love*. After all, these are the feelings that make life meaningful, right? These are what we're really after. You can activate these energies, this spirit, to find happiness and exhilaration, as well as your truth and power.

I will show you how to use the energy of your thoughts – and of your entire being – to rewire your brain, rediscover your dreams and goals, heal your heart, fulfill your highest mission and create the life you've always fantasized about. How? By transforming your inner reality and understanding your greatest superpower: your energy.

Think of it like this: as children, we're valiant and fearless in going after our dreams. We're propelled forward through some combination of curiosity, vitality and blind faith. Sometimes, though, that natural enthusiasm and conviction can diminish. Naysayers tell us that our ambitions are beyond us. Everyday concerns can consume us. We have bills to pay, appointments to rearrange, children to raise whose own lives and aspirations have potentially been overturned or rearranged by life's tragedies, video conferences that devour our focus and more uncertainty than we've ever known before. We stop chasing our dreams and shelve them just to survive, frequently without realizing it.

I was no stranger to simply tolerating things as they were and allowing disappointments to lead the way. I've been there – but I'm here now with this book for you, because I want to share how I got out of feeling stuck, unfulfilled and really low and arrived at a place of, well, magnificence. No matter where you are or what you've gone through, it's still possible to alter your life and see your dreams come true. I did it and I've since helped thousands of other people to do it too. And now, I want to help you.

Maybe you lost your dreams long ago because society told you you'd never make it, that you weren't good enough or smart enough or *whatever* enough. Or perhaps you've just awakened to a fresh dream because you had no choice but to feel the fear bubbling up inside and listen to a new voice.

That's the thing about energy and vibrations, purpose and transformation. It's always relevant; it's just that some of us are ready to hear it before others. Some of us need to go through a few dark nights of the soul to be able to listen. Life, in those moments, can be something to endure rather than a gift to relish.

One of the most powerful turning points in my journey was when I heard a whisper inside telling me there was *more* – and that I was running out of time to grab it.

But what was that *more* that I needed to find?

After some inner squabbling – and outer screaming – I realized this: I wanted to do something bigger than just exist.

It was that basic. It was also that profound.

However vast my discontent may have been, it was matched by my drive to find a solution to my pain. A way out that meant more than my individual comfort, and a way forward that would generate a different kind of joy – and one that wasn't just my own. I started looking where I hadn't looked before: in spirituality and in science. And I realized that together they can be used to discover – and manifest – our dreams, including those we left behind in childhood or the ones that were stolen from us during the COVID trauma or from the cultural conditioning of "being realistic."

I've always been intrigued by energy and the part it plays in our happiness and everyday life. Using the right energetic tools, I, you, we *all* can co-create on an individual and global level that will benefit us greatly. *Quantum Vibes* is the outcome of my search, the signpost showing the way out of our common struggles.

What if you knew that the universe really does have your back (even when it doesn't look or feel like it), and that your life can be dramatically influenced by the energy of your thoughts and emotions? What if you knew that turning up your inner vibrational frequency could help you break through the glass ceilings you've been shrinking under for decades? What if you knew that, with consistent, conscious effort, you could raise your vibrational energy – and draw into your life the passion, purpose and freedom you've long sought?

The second I started to understand the way energy works, I had a massive transformation. The more I delved into the latest research on neuroscience, the more information I found confirming we *do* have the power to change our thought patterns, beliefs and general outlook. All of this altered my life and opened my heart to the grace, pleasure and satisfaction I had been pursuing. It also led me to where I am today: at the top of my game, in service to others and living a life defined by my soul's mission.

I don't pretend to be perfect, or not to be affected by the ups and downs of life. Of course I am; we all are. I've definitely had my fair share of hopping on the hot-mess express. I'm still having good days and bad days just like everyone else. But what I am doing differently from what others are maybe able to do is I'm tapping into the tools that got me to where I am today – and I do so again and again. I am answering the deepening call I am feeling to help humanity not just get back on its feet but to feel amazing and full of hope and excitement again. Since you are here, it looks like you're ready to join me on this journey. Congratulations, get pumped and prepare to build a life that will blow your mind!

Girl Awakened

"The wound is the place where the Light enters you."

Rumi

I spent the first 30 years of my life searching for a feeling. A feeling of joy, of freedom, of meaning, of connection. But no matter where I looked or how many pairs of designer shoes I crammed into my closet, I couldn't find it.

I'd been a go-getter from day one. By the time I hit 31, I had the sort of life I'd desired. I had the job. I had the house. I had the clothes, the car, the posse. I also had the boyfriend, who was *this close* to popping the question.

By that point in my life, I'd spent the better part of my adulthood consulting with topnotch hospitals and training surgeons on new technologies and devices used in operating rooms. The devices I worked with, the technologies I saw, the miracles I witnessed daily – they all fascinated me. I loved being a part of something that helped people have a second chance.

But the X-rays and MRIs and ultrasounds I was surrounded by also showed me that what we present to the outside world can differ wildly from what's happening internally. The body can seem perfectly healthy from the outside but, when you get a glimpse of what is going on internally, you can see things that you just couldn't see before.

That dissonance resonated with me – a bit too much – because I understood that the same thing was true of the mind and the emotions. There was a huge clash between what I showed to the world and what lurked invisible, underneath. On the outside, everything didn't look just okay – it looked *awesome*. Most days I was excelling at work and adding more zeroes to my savings account. Many nights I was dining at the newest, hottest restaurant and tossing back fancy champagne at nightclubs with swanky zip codes. Many weekends I was air-bound, away on luxury trips with my almost-fiancé and entourage of friends. My future was bright, and so was my present.

There Had to Be More

The problem was, when the lights were off and the music had stopped and my make-up was washed off, I was slammed with a realization so stunning I didn't want to face it. *I wasn't enjoying this.* Those quick moments of bliss, the string of prestigious sales reward trips I'd won, the trendy clothes that hugged my butt in precisely the right way – sure they were fun, even tantalizing, but I couldn't help thinking there had to be *more* out there. It felt like I was eternally chasing after something that kept slipping around the corner before I could even get to the end of the street. Away from the lights and action, away from everything I had once thought was everything I wanted, I was, frankly, depressed.

I tried to avoid it. I was busy being busy. I refused to sit still or be alone for long, because that meant being quiet and getting real with what was happening inside me.

Like many people who are new to this whole soul-emergence thing (and may be flailing around like I once did), I decided to renovate my life from the outside in. I started with my house. I wanted something bigger and more beautiful – and who says you have to wait to do nice things for yourself? The things I wanted, such as safety, light, freedom, space, nourishment and nature, I put into my remodelling plan. It would look like this, I told myself: a fancy new garage, casement windows, 10-foot-high ceilings, a deluxe kitchen and an enormous cedar deck overlooking the forest behind my home.

The Downward Spiral

But then I ended my relationship with the man I'd been sure I'd marry. I boomeranged right into a rebound relationship. He appeared perfect on paper: smart, sweet, successful, accomplished, and from a good, fun-loving family to boot. But I still had to shush the voices inside me that said *something's not quite right here*. And I don't mean the paint colour I chose for the kitchen.

Meanwhile, my remodel turned into a nightmare and I was suddenly thigh-high in debt. My home had no roof for a time, rendering it uninhabitable, and its interior – kind of like my own inner world – was covered in mounds of sawdust. My rebound boyfriend invited me to stay with him but he lived in a bachelor pad with two room-mates, a sink perpetually full of dishes and a shared bathroom. Not *quite* my style. I couch-surfed at all my married friends' houses and began to unravel. The box I was trying to fit my life into didn't have my name on it, and all of the efforts I'd made to squeeze into its confines were blowing up in my face.

At the same time, work started to feel false and distant, as if another girl on autopilot was finishing her daily tasks that had in the past earned her promotions and company-wide respect. My confidence dwindled along with my savings. The new boyfriend and I called it quits over Pinot and pizza and, while I knew the break up was the right thing to do, it still felt like a sucker punch to the stomach. I wanted the whole shebang – a husband, two children, maybe even a goldendoodle puppy. My heart sank as I realized I'd be "starting over" yet again.

A friend offered me a furnished condo while she was away, which was a relief, but the move arrived with a new kind of loneliness. Clubbing now triggered a seemingly unfillable longing and so I took to drinking by myself to get through the evenings. When that proved to be insufficient, I started supplementing my Pinot with Xanax.

The bubbly girl I'd been disappeared with the bottles I tossed into recycling.

My Quantum Moment

One afternoon in my friend's echoing town house, I stared at the clock on my phone, willing it to be 5pm already so I could pour myself a glass of wine with at least a modicum of respectability. It had to be the longest 4:59 in history. When 5pm hit, I got up to uncork the bottle and felt my entire body trembling. My palms were sweaty. Every part of my being felt distraught. Tears began to stream down my face. I took a giant, deep breath because a yoga teacher once taught me to do so, and for the first time – well, ever – I started paying attention to a different feeling, the one in the pit of my stomach and the voice that accompanied it.

This isn't the woman you are meant to be, it said. *This is not what you came here to do. There is so much more for you. You are* meant *for so much more!* I could feel the words as if they were being shouted from the rooftops. They were so loud and undeniable, I had no choice but to listen.

And so I did listen, but I also had no idea what to do about what I heard. I'd had faith since I was a child and so, in that moment, I dusted it off, got down on my knees (literally), with tears streaming down my cheeks, and asked

God and the universe to show me a new way of being, to help me remember what it was I came here to accomplish.

I tried to bargain with myself at first. I tried to trick myself into believing that maybe, just maybe, my life with its lack of genuine meaning was fine as it was, because it takes strength and willpower to tune into our divine internal monologue. The whisper only got more defiant – yet also more alluring. Because it reminded me of what I've known since childhood: that I – like you – am here to do something remarkable. To exist on a deeper, more gratifying and transcendent plane. And the quantum shift in my life began in that very special quantum moment that changed the trajectory of my life forever.

That's the thing about the universe and life itself – the universe answers. And the lower it lets us fall, the higher it also allows us to soar.

Yes, soaring *higher* is what this book is about. *Quantum Vibes* is a call not only for getting your foot up on the first rung of the ladder but for seizing the top. It's a guide to help you blow past the hurdles that have stopped you in your tracks and help you dive into the happiness and purpose that is waiting for you, just as it was waiting for me.

Where and how, you might ask? Through soul connection and vibrations on a whole new level. Through using your vibration to create your reality instead of allowing your reality to create your vibration. To feel life as it was meant to be, brimming with delight and significance.

Finding My Life Purpose

I'd looked for "that feeling" in romantic relationships. I'd looked for it in career accomplishments. I'd looked for it in Bloomingdale's and Prada and, in my twenties, every nightclub east of the Mississippi. But the one place I hadn't gone searching was in two realms that had both stumped me: science and spirituality.

Placing those words side by side might make some people gasp. If so, I know how you feel. I grew up in Georgia, and the South is one of the most religious parts of the USA. But I also grew up in the 90s, when the division between religion and science in school, as well as in society, was sharp. Trying to explain spirituality with science can be daunting, but finding the spiritual lessons in science? Now we're talking.

As I sobbed through that afternoon and fought against my desire to numb it all away, the voice inside me said it was up to me to find a way to gain access to that feeling I was after – and it was that intersection between science and spirituality that held the answer.

I stumbled upon Gary Zukav's *The Seat of the Soul* (and by stumbled, I mean I saw it on Oprah's Instagram page) and was struck by him mentioning that all of our souls have a plan and a purpose before we're even born into a human body. I was blown away. Life. Purpose. *Life purpose.* Why had I never considered that *this* was the feeling I was desperate for? How had I completed years of education, travelled to exotic places, bought and renovated a home, nailed a great career and yet *still* hadn't been aware of this? I mean a life purpose is what you're born to do, right? As in the purpose of your life!

I became a woman on a mission. I started researching happiness. Truth. Authenticity. Intuition. The power of aligning your personality with your soul; self-compassion and self-love. The idea that we can draw into our lives exactly what we need and want through the Law of Attraction – meaning, if we create high vibes in our life, we receive high vibes in return. These words were a foreign language to me, but I devoured books that gifted me with ideas for a major life change. Finally, I was excited about something again!

Along the way, I discovered the works of David R Hawkins, a psychiatrist who was also a pioneer in the science of consciousness and spirituality. Before I knew it, I was missing Saturday sales at Neiman Marcus and trying to internalize Hawkins's Map of Consciousness, which demonstrates how powerful our thoughts are, from the depressing and gloomy feelings a global pandemic can evoke to the higher-frequency, lift-you-up thought patterns of optimism and forgiveness. Hawkins explained how these thoughts translate into energies that directly influence our lives, minds and bodies, intersecting as they do with the quantum field of energy. This allowed me to understand even more clearly – even viscerally – how we can change our minds and lives through simple changes to our thoughts. The map opened up the physical reality of quantum physics in a way that showed me the practical and inspiring possibilities of working with it.

You may be thinking, what is this quantum thing? You may have heard the word "quantum" tossed around. Maybe you've even taken a quantum leap – a phenomenon we'll delve into later in the book. Perhaps you've been intrigued by all the talk about quantum computing, watched the TV series or played the video game, *Quantum Break*.

How to Measure and "Vibe Up" Your Energy

The Hertz Vibration Scale (*see* opposite) is a visual representation of energy that taught me how to "vibe up" my world, both internally and externally. Not to go all Sheldon Cooper on you, but this scale measures waves of energy. We'll work with this scale throughout the book. In doing so, it will make it easy for you to vibe with your dreams in an amazingly effective way. Once you grasp the basics of energy, you'll realize it's a super-easy concept that proves you can create anything – and I mean anything – you desire by intentionally utilizing the vibrations of your thoughts and feelings. Yep, I'm talking post-COVID-19 success (way bigger than anything you ever imagined before the crisis), soul-expanding love and that dream job you know you're destined for.

THE HAWKINS HERTZ SCALE

Hz	
700+	Enlightenment
600	Peace
540	Joy
500	Love
400	Reason
350	Acceptance
310	Willingness
250	Neutrality
200	Courage
175	Pride
150	Anger
125	Desire
100	Fear
75	Grief
50	Apathy
30	Guilt
20	Shame

Higher Frequency

Lower Frequency

Do I have your attention with this scale? Good. It's based on the pioneering work of David R Hawkins and his Map of Consciousness (see page xxiii).

Now, think back to high school science, when we learned that Einstein once said that everything in life is vibration. This is because everything is comprised of atoms. And atoms are in a perpetual state of motion, from the sofa you sit on to watch your favourite TV series to the car or subway seat where you might be reading or listening to this book. Sound is also a vibration. So are your thoughts, which is perhaps the most important thing to note in terms of igniting your dream life.

Have you ever walked into a room and immediately felt what can only be described as *good* energy? Maybe you felt a warm, happy vibration that you couldn't totally identify but knew was there. Or maybe you felt inspired or excited. That was energy flowing! That was you feeling the vibrations, the frequencies that were in that room. They were high vibes.

On the other hand, have you ever stepped into a room that had bad energy? A room that, even if it had good lighting and posh furniture, felt dark and glum and heavy? Nothing bad has even happened to *you* there, but you just know there's something shady about the place. Those are "bye" ("get me out of here") vibes – or low and dense energy at work.

The same goes with people. You've probably met some who were inexplicably captivating. In whose presence you were convinced that, no matter your belief system, they were radiating some sort of magnetic, fabulous energy. (Of course you have – this is one of the first steps to falling in love.)

On the flipside, have you ever met someone who, no matter the solid reputation that preceded them or the chic clothes they were sporting, exuded a heaviness that told you to make a run for it?

You feel high energy and you feel low energy, and you can also *be* high energy and low energy. This is what I'm talking about. This is what the scale shows.

Let me show you a little more of what I mean. You intentionally tune in to a specific frequency and then you receive that frequency in return, just as you tune in to a specific channel to see *The Voice*, just as you can tune in to Spotify and hear your boyfriend's mix of the Stones and

Maroon 5. (Go figure.) These are invisible waves at work, based on a frequency. We use these frequencies as signals *all day long*, every time we connect to Wi-Fi, FaceTime or get swipe happy on Hinge.

And everyone, you included, can deliberately create a feeling – a vibration inside your being that is a match for your dreams.

Yes, you heard me right. You have the power to create high-vibration experiences and situations based on the thoughts you think and the vibration you are, consequently, emitting. Everything that comes to be in your life can be due to the vibration of your thoughts and the energy you're both calling into your being and expressing to others. How? Because as quantum physics shows us, on a subatomic level everything in the universe is composed of vibrating energy.

You can use the Hertz Vibration Scale (*see* page xxv) to calibrate the vibrations your emotions produce. One of the reasons I love this scale is because it adds a feeling of tangibility to energy. If you are baking a cake, you have a recipe that tells you to measure one cup of sugar and what to do with it. This scale shows you a way to measure energy. While energy can be subjective and it definitely changes throughout the day, it's very powerful when we can begin to become aware of where we are "vibing" in relation to the scale.

Look at the scale on page xxv, then close your eyes and take a deep breath – where do you think you are on the scale at this moment? Most likely you are at least at the willingness or acceptance stage because you are reading this book. Maybe you've been feeling really excited and open-hearted lately and are closer to the love zone than you think. Or maybe it's been a rough couple of days, weeks, months or even years, and you are feeling stuck in the fear zone on the scale. There is no right or wrong and there is no exact way to know for sure. It's more about creating an awareness and an opening with your mind and your energy and starting a conversation about one of the most powerful tools you have available to you. Your energy, your vibes!

The emotions you feel and the thoughts you think emanate a vibration, an energy. You can intentionally tune in to a particular frequency and receive that frequency in return. For example, if you tune in to "Peace" you may experience a sense of contentment. This is the universe having your back when you nurture it with love and positivity. On the other hand, by not managing your thoughts, you may let out bad vibes that can attract bad juju right back to you, as it's mirroring your inner world.

As you can see from the scale, some of the lowest frequencies we encounter are shame, grief and fear – the very emotions I was struggling with and that were compelling me to deaden myself with daily drinking at "happy" hours. (In retrospect, these were very, very unhappy hours.) These lower vibrational frequencies were keeping me from radiating the light I was born with. (Side note: We all have this light and we always have access to this light.) The highest frequencies are the antithesis of low vibes, and they're the ingredients to a life that will set your soul on fire: gratitude, excitement, joy, peace and love. The more you tune in to this top tier (500 Hz and above) on the Hertz Vibration Scale, the more your life will unfurl with the passion and pleasure we all have the right to experience. Many of us are feeling a deeper need than ever to align with our true dreams and purpose. Meaning, it's the perfect time to start scaling the scale until you rise. Until you find *your* bliss and purpose.

Turns out that a huge part of my purpose was – and is – to learn how to engage in the highest frequency possible and to show others how to do the same. The more I focused on turning my thoughts toward what's beautiful and right about life, the more I realized the power I had to flip the script and attain happiness.

Introducing the 7 Quantum Tools

In the midst of climbing out of my own dark night of the soul, I was desperate to find joy and meaning and purpose. I was at the point where I would do just about anything to feel connected and loved again. As we go through this book, I'll share with you the voyage I took to crawl out of this bleak hole and how I discovered the 7 Quantum Tools to help me (and later my students and clients) create a life that continues to blow my mind – and often leaves me speechless.

This is how it will go:

- The first Quantum Tool, **Turn Up Your Vibrational Frequency,** serves as the umbrella under which the other six Quantum Tools rest. This tool is beyond powerful because you can turn it up no matter where your starting point is.
- From there, I will show you how to **Connect to the Quantum Field**, the second Quantum Tool. This will help you see the vastness of the universe's infinite possibilities – and how this connection is the golden ticket to taking a quantum leap right into a life that will leave you (joyfully) breathless.
- Next you will learn how to **Align with Love or Above**. This third Quantum Tool will show you how engaging in the energetic frequencies above "Love" on the Hertz Vibration Scale will not only help you tap into the jetstream of success and abundance but will also lead to a higher collective consciousness as more and more of us understand and attune to the vibe of love energy. This tool will help you drop whatever fears you have been holding onto. This is a huge move in the direction of our evolution as a species (and toward a more compassionate, happy and peaceful world).
- The fourth Quantum Tool will show you how to **Reprogram and Rewire Your Mind** by intentionally and unswervingly rewriting the script of your

life through working with your conscious and subconscious minds.

- Then you'll move on to the fifth Quantum Tool to **Repurpose Your Energy** by turning the things that trigger you into a powerful way to manifest magic and new possibilities.
- The sixth Quantum Tool will help you **Activate Your Vision *In The Now*** to dive deep into the quantum field and positively alter your present.
- And finally I'll show you how to use the seventh Quantum Tool, **Follow the Flow of Synchronicity and Divine Guidance**, to stop resisting the natural flow of the universe and instead get directly in its divine current to receive your truest and deepest wishes.

Each of these tools is illuminated through my personal flops and feats, as well as through the anecdotes of clients I've assisted as a transformational mentor. And each of these tools is designed to help you achieve a life that will blow your mind – even on a daily basis!

I'm not pretending that it's easy or that it will all happen overnight. (You might have "quantum moments," which we'll get into. But just briefly, a quantum moment is an abrupt, memorable awakening, even bigger than a Eureka or Aha! moment, that changes your life.) Understanding how your energy affects your reality can and will shift everything – and I mean *everything* – for you.

Remember this: you are bones, tendons, organs, cells – physical, indisputable, wonderful matter. But you are also a soul that needs to unite with your dreams and energy. When you achieve this, you too will discover what I did. Which is this: I put down that bottle of wine and tossed the bottle of pills. I got busy connecting to people who needed more than a good financial retirement plan and Apple TV to be happy. I learned about the overlaps of spirituality and science and began adopting practices that connect the physical brain to positive states of optimism, love and illumination. And I started seeing the real results of the Law of Attraction because I worked to live in sync with the highest vibrations.

I've since coached thousands of people on uncovering and engaging with their purpose, and manifesting their own big, wild dreams. They've become happier, healthier, more prosperous and more in touch with their whole reason for living.

Quantum Vibes is a compilation of all that I've learned. In Part 2 you'll find a workbook of exercises to enable you to put the theory into practice and guide you into the world of boundless opportunities. Why? Because it's your birthright to realize your desires – and, in the end, to reach that high-vibe state.

PART ONE

THE 7 QUANTUM TOOLS

1

Turn Up Your
Vibrational Frequency

*"Your heart has a powerful little antenna and its
vibrations can be felt throughout the universe."*

Suzy Kassem

QUANTUM TOOL #1

Look at where you are in life and take it to the next level. Turn
up the vibration of the energy you're emitting by feeling your
feelings and focusing on the good that is directly in front
of you.

Say Hi, Vibes

In the summer of 2019, I had a moment. Like, a real moment. I was eating breakfast in the mountains of Lake Garda, Italy, staring out at one of the most gorgeous vistas I'd ever seen, when my heart almost burst. *Could anything be more beautiful?* I asked myself. Could this *really* be my life?

And then it hit me: *I* created this. Not the glistening lake, not the infinity pool, not the lush mountains in the distance, not even (definitely not even) the frittata or the cappuccino in front of me. But the feeling inside me, the energy I was emanating, the location-free career I had that was helping thousands and fuelling my soul along with it – that was because of me and the process I was consciously following.

Clearly, a force much larger than me had a big hand in all of this. But I'd captured this awesome moment by grasping what I feel is the most vital, applicable principle of quantum physics: that we are all made of energy – pure, positive, glorious energy – that vibrates according to the intention and feeling and thought we put into it. This gives us the opportunity to swing to a higher frequency to start creating the life we've long been craving.

To some, this is empowering. To others, it's unnerving, as it puts the onus squarely on us – and let's be real, it's a legit responsibility. Indeed, going from that girl with a wine o'clock habit to the woman sipping cappuccino

4

in the Italian mountains was painful at times. In the beginning it was slow-moving and frustrating as I tried to internalize, really internalize, the notion that we're all energy and that it's our duty to own this, work with this and *be* it. After all, it's so much easier to cozy on down with a bottle of red, self-pity and Netflix than it is to try to understand how the universe works and put in the effort to keep yourself faithful, connected, curious, engaged and committed.

Quantum physics was my entry point to this new way of being. The old paradigm suggests that matter emits energy, which, truth be told, can leave a girl feeling pretty helpless. Quantum physics, on the other hand, turns this concept on its head and tells us that, nope, we had it wrong: energy *creates* matter.

What does this mean? Excitingly, it means that tree in your yard from a before-awakened perspective looks barren. Blink and see it again, and the tree has buds that are priming to bloom next season. It means that those neighbours, from a before-awakened experience, appear to be driving you crazy by sonically assaulting the neighbourhood with their karaoke. Listen again and, hey, you actually really love their rendition of that Whitney Houston song and feel like grooving to it! It means that it seems that no one, in your before-awakened perspective, is keen on you; that there isn't a man or woman who even casts a glimpse your way, let alone asks for your number. Look again, and you'll find that the world is teeming with opportunities to connect with high-vibe souls who are ready to rock your world.

"Awakening" might be confusing here, even off-putting. I get it: it tends to suggest an intense, ecstatic, almost-leap-up-from-a-wheelchair experience, which I'm not disparaging, but it's not the awakening I'm talking about. I'm talking about awakening to the knowledge that the energy we match our internal vibrational frequency to determines the outcome and experience of our life. I'm talking about the power and necessity of consistently elevating your thoughts to raise the world around you – and, importantly, to uplift the world inside yourself. This is the key to restoring a life you may have lost or to finding the life you have longed for – to grow.

I said yes to growth and kept saying yes and *still* say yes. Besides, life is less about discovering yourself than it is about *inventing* yourself. Or rather, deliberately creating a reality that electrifies you on a daily basis.

Of course, I don't always know how my goals will materialize. I'm not always confident I won't fall flat on my face as I chase them, either. In fact, I'm willing to fail over and over again, because that's part of the process to reach real success, however you define it. But I do always know that I have to follow my heart and soul. And my heart tells me that I need an elevated attitude – a high vibrational feeling – period.

Amplifying Your Vibrational Frequency with Quantum Tool #1

With the first of my Quantum Tools, **Turn Up Your Vibrational Frequency,** I am going to teach you, to show you, how to boost your vibrations so you can begin to consciously create whatever it is that you have been secretly dreaming of but maybe haven't let yourself say out loud yet. In a nutshell, you are an energetic being who emits a frequency. You create your very own vibration. And the vibration you emit dictates the life you're living.

Dr Joe Dispenza phrases this notion differently when he says, "The quantum field" (which we'll dive into in Tool #2) "responds not to what we want; it responds to *who* we are being."

If we're being all doom and gloom, if we're dedicating our time and energy to focusing on external things that vex us, if we're feeling low and hopeless – well, it kinda sorta always regulates how everything looks and feels and seems and *is* around us. This is especially important when we are faced with a global or personal crisis. We have a tendency to let our exterior reality affect our vibration.

But if we're tapped into the higher notes on the Hertz Vibration Scale (see overleaf) and thinking serenely, hopefully and joyfully, regardless of what our current circumstances are, life outside begins to take on a lovelier and way more exciting hue. Life, inside, no longer feels

THE HAWKINS HERTZ SCALE

Hz	
700+	Enlightenment
600	Peace
540	Joy
500	Love
400	Reason
350	Acceptance
310	Willingness
250	Neutrality
200	Courage
175	Pride
150	Anger
125	Desire
100	Fear
75	Grief
50	Apathy
30	Guilt
20	Shame

Higher Frequency

Lower Frequency

angry, hopeless, frustrated and fragmented. It feels coherent, open, willing and ready. It's that light I saw in meditation with a reiki healer (see page 18) that first made me feel a ray of wonder and love and possibility. This Quantum Tool has served me and many of my clients very well throughout times of fear, uncertainty and massive change.

Let's take a look at the scale again.

Got it? Good.

As already mentioned, every living and breathing thing on the planet – from that plant on your windowsill to that off-the-shoulder romper you're wearing, to the hope that you are holding onto in this very moment as you read this – breaks down into small (like, really, really small) particles. And each of these particles has a specific energetic quality.

Some call this a vibration, others a frequency. And that energy changes with the energy *we* apply to it.

Think of classic Newtonian physics: drop a glass on the floor and it'll likely shatter. Push a chair hard enough and it'll fall over. Go pedal to the metal and, hey, you made it to your destination with time to spare.

Now consider quantum physics, which says that everything is energy, and think of how you can work this *in your favour*. For example, Einstein proved that $E = mc^2$ – that energy is the equivalent to mass (which is matter) times the speed of light. In other words, energy and matter are just two different forms of the same thing. Any little bit of matter can be transformed into a huge amount of energy. This means that you have enormous personal potential simply through vibing up your energy. Ivan Young, PhD, says that emotion is energy plus motion – or E-Motion. In other words, "The more energy you pour into anything, the more of that thing you receive."

If someone had tried to tell me this a decade ago, I would've rolled my eyes and muttered *obviously* in the other direction. And yet if I'd taken a step back and seen how this straightforward but great law of nature applied to me, I would have been appalled. There I was, healthy in body and bank account, but stuck in the loop of victimhood: I had no home, no true love, no focus or fulfillment. I was pouring all of my energy and motion into telling myself the same sad story over and over again, perpetuating my own dismal reality. I felt stuck, disappointed and resentful and I had no idea that I, and I alone, had the power to change this.

This process of recognizing (and, later, maneuvering) energy is largely intuitive. If you spend your energy on, say, yoga or dance or even mathematics, there's a really good chance you'll master it. If you allocate your energy to your garden, it'll thrive with blooms, herbs or whatever plants you've chosen. Your energy goes where you focus it. If you are in the car and you aren't jiving with the song on the radio, what do you do? You change the dial, tune into a different frequency and hear a different song. You can do this with your thoughts and your energy too. You turn up your frequency by changing the dial, shifting your focus and deciding to emit a different frequency that is zeroed in on where you want to go.

Feelings emit frequency, so the higher my frequency, the higher my vibration and the faster and easier my dreams will flow to me. The energy I put out will be matched by what I get back. This means that based on the way that you feel and the thoughts that you think, you are emitting a vibration, an energy that will reflect your outer world.

You intentionally tune in to a specific frequency and then you receive that frequency. If you are reading or listening to these words, then you are able to intentionally create a feeling, a vibration that is a match for your dreams. You can intentionally tune into the feeling of what you desire. And your job is to always look at engaging the highest frequency possible.

This is where the Law of Attraction also begins to come into play. Like matches like, and things grow and expand where energy flows. You can intentionally tune in to the feeling of what you desire – and then literally watch how the world changes around you in kind.

Believe in Murphy's Law, and everything that can go wrong will go wrong. Believe in Yhprum's Law, yep that's a thing – the opposite of Murphy's Law (in fact, it's Murphy's spelled backward) – and everything that *can* work will work.

In any given moment we have two options: to step forward into growth and the unknown or backward into the feeling of certainty which, for most of us, is in those rehearsed states of being that have kept us on the low-end of the Hertz Vibration Scale. Here, we experience lower-vibe emotions such as dread, anxiety, resentment and jealousy. Step into the growth mindset where the higher vibes rest and the world starts delivering. Expansion versus contraction. Persevering versus cowering. Loving versus fearing.

When I say turn up your vibration, I don't mean in just a simple up-or-down way; I mean create a bigger, more expanded energy. When you turn up the volume on your TV or radio, it's true that the sound becomes louder, but it also reaches further and wider. Think of your energy in this way too. We live in a world full of dense vibrations and when we turn up our own vibration, the true magic is being able to hold the higher frequencies at the same time as maybe we are feeling some shame or fear, without letting the lower-vibe emotions take the driver's seat. I will explain more about this in Tool #5 when I share one of my favourite and most impactful exercises to make room for the many dynamic feelings you will experience on this journey to fulfillment.

While I messed up more times than I can count, one thing I've always done, even before I was "aware" or conscious of a better way of being, was to always look on the bright side. This has served me well, and now that I understand the power of mindset and how thoughts become things, it gives optimism and appreciation an entirely new importance.

It is that imperative – and it's also that simple. When we get so caught up in the bad stuff in front of us that isn't working – and concentrate on that and only that – we get more, well, bad stuff. Traffic is endless. Payments are late. More lay-offs are coming. The pandemic will never end. That latte you just bought spills all over your car seat. When we focus on the fact that our partner is disappointing us, we bristle with an energy that shifts how they relate to us and they either pull away or get angry, which disappoints and angers us even more. When we give in to a bad mood, we lower the moods of those around us too. Doom begets doom begets doom.

However, if we can always try to see a silver lining and choose a better, elevated thought, emotion and behaviour – and make this our MO, our 24/7 experience. We can start to shift negativity in an instant by turning up our vibes, and then the world around us does too. Traffic opens up for us. Payments arrive on time. Not being in a relationship and even quarantine can feel like a gift of mental and physical spring cleaning. And that latte is thanks to that hottie ahead of you in line, who bought it for you while you were checking out all the good news on your iPhone. The hurts of our past and present don't vanish, of course, but the now starts shining a little brighter and the future starts to glimmer with hope. We, in turn, start gliding toward it.

Indeed, when we apply optimism on a conscious, steady basis, the world transforms. Chances are, you will not become a millionaire overnight or wake up to the job of your dreams. (Well, maybe ... it certainly isn't off the table). But you will begin to savour what you have right now in front of you in a mighty state of appreciation, while also being grateful for where you're headed. With this in hand, you will be on the express lane to that life you have forever fantasized of having.

Michelle Changes Her Energy – and Her Life

I met Michelle for the first time at a retreat I hosted in Sedona, Arizona. Her soul wasn't in a good place, in spite of the stunning beauty all around us. Amid those amazing red-rock structures, she looked every bit the girl boss with her black matte Gucci flats, Kate Spade briefcase and bouncy hair. She moved through the room like she owned it. But as she sat down with me, she said that all that self-assurance was a façade. Deep down, everything about her, from the condo she owned in the San Francisco Bay Area to the Prius she drove, was more or less just window dressing. (*That's* how down she was on herself.) As a marketing executive at a beauty company, she was surrounded by models who looked like they subsisted on hemp milk lattes and aroma-diffused air. She commuted two hours every day, spending her time on the road listening to the "morose voices" of NPR news and getting upset about the state of the world, while her children grew ever closer to their nanny. As a single mother, she only saw her kids first thing in the morning and late in the evening. She'd bring home Thai takeout or pizza for dinner for herself (as they'd already eaten with their nanny), tuck them into bed, read to them for a bit and then hit her MacBook again to keep her edge in the workplace and to dull the mom guilt she felt for hardly seeing them.

On weekends, she'd chauffeur her kids to sporting events and scroll through her social media channels after they were asleep, annoyed and resentful at the posts about the vibrant lives others appeared to be living. She had a few women she considered friends, but in recent months hadn't made an effort to reach out to them, in part because they were relentlessly competitive and bragged about everything from their vacation houses to their preschoolers' acceptance into exclusive schools.

She wasn't depressed – she'd seen two therapists to confirm this – but she wasn't excited about life, either. She was operating on autopilot. She felt like she was living to work, instead of working to live. Time seemed to be slipping by. "My children will be grown up and out of the house before I know it," she said. "And what am I doing it for – to keep up with the Joneses?"

In other words, she was, in many ways, like me, BA – Before Awakening. Feeling a lacklustre level of excitement about life and a deep knowing that there had to be more *out there*.

Sometimes in life, I told Michelle, we get wrapped up in things that don't really matter, like if Chloe's mom is a better, more present mother or if you're not *enough* as a woman or why you can't fit into the new black dress you just bought. Like me, Michelle felt like she had checked so many boxes, and she *still* wasn't feeling happy or fulfilled. And, like me, she felt that there was something more out there but had no idea where "there" was or how she could find it.

Michelle admitted she was on the low end of the vibration scale, and I could see it. She was turning her vibes down instead of up. And the more I got her to *open* up, the more I realized that she needed to do some inner rewiring. She wanted a spiritual connection, genuine friends and an awesome relationship with her children, and to feel proud of her body and achievements. And yet she was stuck on a channel, a frequency, that wasn't just not serving her, it was destroying her wellbeing. Picking up the remote and changing the channel to turn up her frequency was the first step to attracting and creating the life she knew she was destined for. What's more, she *had* to do this if she wanted to activate a new reality.

As I told Michelle, you're always going to have an emotion, a feeling, going through you. And the more intentional you become about honouring (and *feeling*) that emotion – that frequency at the highest level – then managing it, the more you will magnetize circumstances and opportunities that mirror it.

The "there" isn't in Paris, the master suite of the penthouse you're coveting or in the arms of Ryan Gosling's doppelganger; nor is it to be found in the promotion you're waiting for or in being the perfect, polished mom who's first in line to pick up her kids and always goes on fieldtrips. The "there" – and this is the scary (but also empowering) part – is right here *inside you*.

Michelle felt that it was too late for her, but I assured her that it was only the start. I created a strategy for her, which reflects what you will find in the subsequent chapters of this book.

First, though, I gave her a number of insights on how she could further nourish her mind and energy, not just in a once-in-a-while way, but on a nearly hourly basis. She could inspire her mind by unfollowing Instagram accounts filled with ego and instead follow people and groups that would lift her spirits. She could stop upsetting herself with listening to the news and find podcasts and audio books that would galvanize her.

I gave her permission to acknowledge and respect her anxiety and anger, and encouraged her to return to her journal or therapy to address these issues. I asked her to stop isolating herself and to work as diligently on finding heartwarming friendships as she did at her career. I urged her to prioritize and pay close attention to what is already working in her life and to being happy – and to keep doing this as long as possible. I persuaded her to carve out time for her children to mitigate her mom guilt and build a lasting emotional connection with the humans she loved so dearly. Most of all, I asked her to concentrate on raising her internal energy and turning up her vibe by focusing on the top tier of the Hertz Vibration Scale (see page xxv). "The more you let yourself do things that bring you joy, the higher you will vibe on the vibration scale," I shared with Michelle. "When you let your heart burst open, life starts to feel rich and rewarding and you begin to turn your vibes up. This could be from a hug and a kiss from your kids or by taking a moment to pause and watch the sunset and allowing time just to stand still. Or it could be if you're enjoying a margarita with that friend who truly just gets you and always tells the funniest stories that have you giggling like a schoolgirl. Yes, you need more of that in your life, starting now," I explained.

Michelle's transformation didn't happen overnight. But her breakthrough began the second she committed to turning up her frequency. Within only a few weeks, she started to see results. Indeed, she told me that she felt better than she ever had before. Her new self-care routine had allowed her to start loving herself and her body again. She felt a bond growing with her children. After a couple of months of implementing this process, she was given the opportunity to work part-time from home. This led to more productive work hours, a more fulfilling personal life and even room to amp up her self-care routine. All of which really did blow her mind!

Becoming "Light-ified"

Long before I'd met Michelle, when I had started jumping into these questions myself, I came across a reiki healer who, I'm convinced, was deliberately placed on my path to put me on the route toward healing and purpose. At the time, I didn't know reiki from reishi (yes, as in the mushroom), but desperate pleas sometimes call for desperate answers. This reiki/reishi healer nearly sent me flying out the door when she asked me to consider what I was doing before I was born.

Um, I had no idea. I wasn't anything; I was hardly a button waiting in my dad's back pocket. Hello, I hadn't even been *born* yet.

She then led me into a meditation and I visualized a light-oozing euphoria beyond anything any hallucinogens or orgasm had ever generated. It was soft, vibrant and all-encompassing. It was peace and potential, personified (or rather, light-ified). I like to think of it as the glow of ecstatic love and limitless possibilities.

As the healer and other sources later told me, this meant that before I was born I had an epic mass of energetic light that could be shaped into what I desired once I was born, on this planet, in the 21st century. (Don't worry, we won't be talking about past lives here, at least not in this book!)

I am not alone in this vision. Just as we all have a body, we also all have a soul, and our wise, timeless, loving soul inhabits our body. Our heart and soul are where our true wisdom resides.

This realization is tricky for some of us to consider because we often cling to the things we identify as: mother, brother, wife, boyfriend, son, daughter; software engineer, lawyer, writer, doctor; blonde, brunette, Japanese, Irish, Greek, whatever. Identification can serve us well at times, but it also puts us in a place where we feel tied to meet preset obligations, causing us to forget about that inherent light completely. And when we do? We only think of "surface" ways to mold that energy of possibilities.

Knowing that I had access to this boundless light and energy inside me didn't mean that I could use it to click my heels and have Naomi Campbell's figure and elegance or Kim Kardashian's cheekbones, or a Ferrari in my garage in a blink. (None of this stuff truly matters, anyway.) But it did mean I could embody the energy by tapping into and channelling a higher, more open and expansive energy that represented the pure grace and love that I already had long before I was born. And I could call upon it again and again to do *good* for myself and for others. I could use it to experience seemingly unending happiness; to know that love would never fade; to have faith in the fact that anything is possible. It tasted like freedom and it felt like change, and by the time I opened my eyes in that reiki healer's treatment room, I realized that I would devote the rest of my life to capturing that feeling again and again, no matter what it required. Why? Because I'd found a new brand of magic – and I was convinced it was going to take me places.

I don't mean the magic of fairies and dragons here, although those work for some. I don't mean the magic of Vegas, either, where trickery and illusions rule. No, I mean the magic of lifting the veil and looking at life through a fresh pair of eyes and seeing all the treasures and potential that rests in our very own energy field. In our own light.

Magic happens when you start to tune in to high vibes. Invisible doors open, synchronicities are abundant and that uncomfortable, sometimes all-consuming feeling of wondering if there is more to life vanishes. Don't get me wrong – as I said, it's not all peaches and roses, especially in the beginning. There may be more of an internal struggle than robust internal strength and the glee that comes with it. It's also not simply a matter of putting on rose-coloured glasses and forgetting the hurts, losses and tragedies that inescapably rattle us. Rather, it's calling upon your higher vibe to get through difficulties without losing sight of your ultimate vision, and without lowering the vibration you're emitting. Often when you choose the path of alignment and positivity, your ego or your fears will flare up and do everything in their power to guide you in the opposite direction and keep you off track, but I'll give you the tools throughout this book to combat this. All the more reason why it's crucial to take fast action to shut down the negativity and tune in to a different, higher-vibe channel. Because on an energetic level, the higher the Hertz vibes of your signal, the deeper your lifelong change and the greater your level of enthusiasm and contentment.

To be clear, I am by no means suggesting that you should bypass your feelings or what your heart is telling you if it's not "high vibe." In fact, just the opposite, so stop numbing and start feeling. Such a practice permits you to feel what you *need* to feel in order to ascend. When you embark on the exercises throughout this book, you should give yourself full permission to respect and experience all of your feelings. By doing so with comfort and self-compassion, you will automatically raise your vibes. Turning up your vibes does NOT mean nonchalantly ignoring your feelings and simply tuning into a higher vibe feeling. It means giving yourself grace, empathy and compassion, and allowing your feelings to move through you with love. (More coming on this in Quantum Tool #3, see page 43.)

Turn Up Your Vibrational Frequency – Today

It may sound basic and clichéd – perhaps even crazy – but I created monumental happiness for myself by shifting my overall perspective and energy. What if for even just a minute you could start to do the same by looking at things through a different lens, from a perspective of something much bigger, much different than you might have ever thought of before?

Your energy and focus are your greatest superpowers. What you give attention to grows. This begs the question: *what* are you devoting your time, energy and concentration to? Are there aspects of your life, from your social calendar to your career and where and on what you're spending your money, that are forcing you down rather than up? Our energy goes where our money goes. Are you spending money on things that support your happiness and evolution? Or on things that numb what you are feeling?

On the flip side, what is working for you today, in this very moment? What do you have to be grateful for *right now*? It could be something as simple as a healthy, nourishing lunch or that cool new throw you bought for your sofa. It could be something as grand as a luxury trip on a private yacht or your partner saying, "I love you."

List five things, big or small, that you're appreciating right this minute. Maybe it's the fresh air you're breathing as you read this or the memory of the sweet strawberries you had for lunch, or even the laugh you shared with your bestie the night before.

Now think of three things you have accomplished in the last three to six months. It doesn't matter whether they're grandiose or modest. What matters is that tapping into these achievements makes you feel proud. It could be the fact that you're reading this book with the intention to consciously shift your energy; or maybe you recently completed a difficult project; or you helped out a friend last month. What you want to concentrate on here is feeling pride and gratitude for yourself with your mind, body and soul. All of this will naturally turn up your vibrational frequency and place you on the path toward a beautiful quantum existence.

To take this practice deeper and radically turn up your vibration, you can find more exercises in the Workbook (see page 157).

My recommendation is that you commit to spending seven days digging into and practising each Quantum Tool. You can take longer if you need to and you can always revisit any of the tools at any time. In fact, I encourage you to do so.

QUANTUM TOOL #1
Turn Up Your Vibrational Frequency
RECAP

Look at where you are in life and take it to the next level. Turn up the vibration of the energy you're emitting by feeling your feelings and focusing on the good that is directly in front of you.

Your Blueprint for Positive Change

- Get into the habit of evaluating where you are on the Hertz Vibration Scale at least once a day. Once you have an awareness of where you are, you will begin to make radical shifts in the direction of where you want to go.
- Each day take a few moments to give thanks for things that you are grateful for and for what is working in the moment. The frequency of your gratitude will always turn up your vibration.
- Meditating and body movement are two of the most powerful tools you can use to shift your energy and your vibration. Use them daily or as often as you can.
- Find your tribe! Surround yourself with people and conversations that inspire and elevate you. You are here, which means you are already on the right track.

2

Connect to the Quantum Field

*"When you become comfortable with uncertainty,
infinite possibilities open up in your life."*

Eckhart Tolle

QUANTUM TOOL #2

Focus your energy on your dreams, align your personality with your heart and soul and pay more attention to infinite possibilities instead of all the reasons in front of you that make you think things aren't working – even if those limits are entirely within yourself. And a word of encouragement here: you've got this.

Magnetize Infinite Possibilities

As a little girl, I had long, wild blonde curls and an even wilder imagination. I would daydream about unicorns, fairies and rainbows regularly. In first grade, I even decided to change my name to Rainbow Adams and began writing it on my papers until my pragmatic mother found out and insisted I use my real name. It felt so good to dream, so freeing to be outside in the woods bouncing on the rusty red trampoline and letting my imagination fly around with my body.

One particular daydream has always stayed with me – one in which I had a most wonderful life inside a button house.

"A *button house*?" you might ask. Oh, yes. Every wall of this house was covered with buttons in every shade of the rainbow and of all different sizes. Think of it as button wallpaper that was so dazzling it inspired jaw-dropping awe. The deeper I walked into this magical house, the more I realized that each button represented a unique dream; and when you touched one of the buttons, you were instantly transported into the reality of the dream the button signified. And what gorgeous dreams they were, the sort that carried you to charming, bountiful and exotic places. The unicorns and fairies and rainbows I held in my heart were often there. Oh, the places I went to inside that button house!

Then one day, something drastic happened. A part of me no longer felt free to dream or imagine. I couldn't find my way to the button house, no matter how hard I tried. Instead of listening to my intuition, instead of dancing and flying with my imagination on that rusty red trampoline, I heard naysayers – people who told me that unicorns and fairies were fiction and there was a strictly scientific reason for rainbows. I was tired of being laughed at for my "silly" ideas and my "wild" way of dreaming and thinking. I wanted to feel loved and accepted by others, not ostracized. So, I slowly began to put my imagination on a shelf in the dark, back corners of my mind, where it grew dusty and stale, even atrophied. I started to conform to the norm of what a little girl, teenager and eventually a grown woman should "be." Can you relate?

What I didn't realize I was doing was turning off one of the most powerful gifts I had. That we *all* have. This is the energy of possibility, curiosity and wonder. There's an immeasurable amount of abundance and countless situations we can create in our lives – not just in the third-dimensional realm where our human bodies exist, but in the ever-expanding universe. Imagine walking outside in a rural area on a clear night. You see a thousand stars that light up the sky. Imagine honing in on each star through a telescope and seeing even more stars. We are truly specks of stardust when you think of the vastness of the universe. What I didn't know when I decided to dull my imagination is this: if you want to attract your dreams and turn them into reality, you have to give yourself permission to plug into them energetically. To *believe* that your dreams are, in fact, potential opportunities, if not probabilities.

BA (remember: Before Awakening), I didn't pay much attention to the inventive geniuses behind the contraptions and modern marvels many of us (myself included) take for granted. Planes were basically a tube with wings. Smartphones were essential. Cars – well, they worked by some combination of pipes, motors and mechanical witchery. But after learning about quantum physics – and the astonishing possibilities for all of us – I began thinking differently.

Put it this way: we bow down to contemporary and historical bad-asses, from Steve Jobs to Thomas Edison, from Maya Angelou to Tony Robbins, from Elon Musk to Oprah. And yet, how often do we pause to wonder how these mortals rose to heroic heights? I'm willing to bet they did it by tapping into a realm where infinite possibilities exist and by intentionally aligning their energy to connect to that vision. Who knows if this was done on a conscious or unconscious level, but they did it nonetheless – and the results speak (loudly) for themselves.

There is a gateway to the quantum field that many are not aware of. It all starts with that alignment I've talked about. This was a word that didn't mean very much to me before my awakening. Remember, I was busy being busy and numbing out with a full social agenda, nightclubs and vino. The last thing on my mind back then was alignment or my soul or even manifesting, which meant as much to me at that time as quantum physics. But that changed after I got down on my knees and prayed for direction. I wanted to understand the depths of who I really was. Not just my personality, or my likes and dislikes, but my soul. That light that existed inside long before I was even born.

One of the pivotal moments to creating the Quantum Tools and a life that truly blows my own mind was understanding alignment and its real definition. As I write this, I recall a morning when I was first getting into the crossroads between science and spirituality. The temperature was an idyllic 68°F (20°C) and so I curled up outside on my red sofa. I felt the gentle breeze glide through the oak trees; heard the chirp of birds and watched butterflies dance around the cedar beams above me. I had just picked up a book that changed my life, the one I mentioned earlier: *The Seat of the Soul* by Gary Zukav. I sat straight up. My body flooded with shock and surprise, as if a lightning bolt had just hit my chest (only, I should say, in a *good* way).

Zukav explained that as well as a personality, we also have a soul. I hadn't ever really thought about my soul before. It seemed so foreign, yet so close too. The words I read sent chills through my body and just like that, my awareness shifted and my energy began to become more aligned. My heart opened as I began to have compassion for the version of me that had spent all those years searching for that "feeling" and for purpose in all of the wrong places. Finally, I was on the right track. I was following the path my soul wanted me to take. I was finally walking, one foot at a time, right into "alignment."

Zukav has a different term. He calls it *authentic power.* "When the personality begins to serve your soul, that is authentic power," he writes. This means that you understand your soul's purpose and your passions, and you align your personality with them. Once you do, magic begins to unfold around you. In other words, you open the floodgates to the quantum field and endless possibilities.

I am not saying that alignment is the only way to tap into the quantum field. I am saying it's one of the most powerful ways to access it with ease. It's as if you have just pushed the crème de la crème of buttons in the magical button house of my childhood.

Authentic power, alignment, flow, the jet stream of magic and miracles – are all available to me, to you, to anyone who is reading these words or living and breathing on this planet. Our personality lives in the 3D realm but our soul is multidimensional. When we align the two it makes our personality filled with fifth-dimensional power and opportunities. Infinite possibilities everywhere you turn – this is the quantum field. This is creating and manifesting with your energy, not allowing your reality to guide your energy.

When you align your personality with your soul and create authentic power, life starts to get exciting again, much like it was for me when I was a child and most likely how it was when *you* were young. You become curious, playful, imaginative and totally in touch with your dreams. Once you're here, the colours you see are more vivid. The air feels more invigorating. The sunshine pulsates high vibes right into your body. And you begin to enter a type of flow that didn't exist before you tapped into authentic power and alignment.

Accessing Infinite Possibilities with Quantum Tool #2

This brings us to our second Quantum Tool: **Connect to the Quantum Field**. But what is the quantum field? From a spiritual perspective, I think of the quantum field as the place where Source, God, the universe – or however you might define awe – resides. It's a place of energy and grace where anything can happen; an invisible arena that connects everything material. It's a space in the 5D realm of consciousness where magic and miracles not only occur but are *normal* and frequent. Where we can see ourselves on a big stage, or feel deeply, deeply in love. Where we can see our bank account recover and then flourish. Where we can take a far-fetched, unrealistic idea and turn it into a reality in minutes or even seconds. Where we can see life bigger and better and more exciting, even when coming out of the other side of a tragic pandemic, and where we have never felt so grounded and empowered and safe and inspired.

From a physics perspective, the quantum field can be described as the interaction of the electromagnetic field and the electron field, which transfer energy and momentum between them. However, for our purposes, we don't even need to get our heads around the science, but rather to be able to envision the quantum field in a way that makes sense to us. For some, it may appear as an actual place, complete with stars or even buttons. For others, it may be a literal field, perhaps even one made up entirely of light or sunshine and flowers. It doesn't matter. What matters is that we purposefully and persistently draw on the amazement it evokes, the potential it promises and how the feeling it creates is the key to bringing our dreams to fruition.

Close your eyes for a moment, take a deep breath, and imagine all of your dreams flowing to you with ease. You can even picture a butler delivering them to you on a silver platter! Tap into the feelings it arouses. This is you already onto something.

The quantum field is a place that is in alignment with your big, wild dreams. It's a place where truly ANYTHING is possible. At this point you should be on board with the fact that your body is energy and that you emit a frequency. Understanding that you can anchor your energy into other frequencies will give you a new sense of freedom and power. When you become connected to the energy of what you desire, the universe expands. We are no longer just putting one foot in front of the other, marching forward in a way that can feel mundane and endless, separated from the magic that the universe is comprised of. We *are* energy. Once you realize this, and once you align with the potency this holds, the universe has no choice but to supply you with your desires. Many refer to this as being an energetic match to your dreams, because you magnetically pull the possibilities from the quantum field into your 3D reality.

When we tap into the quantum field we let go of control. We can thrive in the unknown and we don't need to know how or when the thing will appear. We plug our energy into a desire and wait to be shown the next step. This is about wrapping your mind around the idea that if you can dream it, you can have it. (And isn't the promise of this marvellous?)

From Bone Dry to Overflow

I had a client named Ian who came to me at the beginning of the pandemic. He said his business was "bone dry" and had been for months. He was mired in despair but also feeling absolutely frantic. Right away, my intuition told me his energy was disconnected from the whole notion of possibility, the essence of the quantum field. The energy around him and the chaos ensuing across the globe had deeply affected his energy, his frequency and his mindset. Ian, like many others during this time, was allowing the energy around him to control his vibration instead of allowing the energy inside him to intentionally create his vibration.

Ian needed a reminder of his own power. He needed someone to help him believe in prospects again, even magic and dreams and manifested desires. He was ready to try anything to reach and exceed the success he knew, deep down, he was capable of achieving.

I guided Ian through a powerful meditation in which I took him into a space of new possibilities and I have shared this exercise with you in the Workbook (*see* page 157). I helped him see how to connect his energy to where he wanted to go, and then let the 3D reality catch up to him. I showed him how to draw his desires toward him using his energy; to use his energy to create, instead of allowing the energy around him to be the deciding factor of his outcomes.

Ian's business came back to life – and then some. Ian's problem before he started working with me was that he had been plugged into all the things that could go wrong. His energy mirrored his failing business. He was completely focused and entangled with lack and rejection. In turn, that's what he was attracting from the quantum field instead of what he truly desired. He made the energetic shifts I helped him with. He decided to reclaim his power and his beliefs in possibility. He practised the meditation daily to plug into and entangle his energy with what he *did* want. He became an energetic match to more abundance. Then, he took the grounded and practical strategies we came up with to increase his visibility and attract clients and was able to create a consistent monthly income of $30,000 (£22,700) in just a few short months. Ian understood the strength of alignment and the power of plugging into the quantum field after seeing such colossal results and such tangible manifestations and abundance appearing.

A Life-changing Soul Adventure

I always joke that spirit, my soul, got to me through luxury spas. In 2011, while my then-boyfriend was on a golf trip, I said yes to my own adventure with my girlfriend Sally and jetted off to Sedona, Arizona. Back then I had never heard of Sedona, but Sally sent me a picture of the red rocks there – splendid and expansive against that clear-blue desert sky, as if they'd descended from heaven – and I was sold. It was amazing how complete I felt the second I stepped onto the 5-star property where we were staying, as if it was the grown-up version of a location delivered à la carte from my button home. Staring out at the panoramic view of the red rocks' intricate lines and towering shapes, I knew this was somewhere you could be transported. This, I knew, was where dreams were converted into actuality. Every turn was breathtaking, so much so I felt as if I was on a movie set.

"Sally, we have such a packed agenda, how are we going to have time for lunch?" I asked with a giggle as we unpacked.

"Protein bars!" she said with a smile as she pulled a few from her bag.

We only had four nights in this little slice of spiritual paradise, but we were prepared. Our agenda was filled with hikes through and to the tip-top of those stunning red rocks: Cathedral Rock, Bell Tower – yes, please!

My motto when travelling has always been to explore what the locals recommend and, when in Rome ... So we booked tarot card readings. I also booked a reading with a shamanic astrologer, even though those type of things were foreign to me at the time. And of course, a spa day – did I say *spa*? We had treatments galore, from Ayurvedic massages to hot stone treatments to Watsu water therapy – we spoiled ourselves rotten and I loved every second of it!

Although the entire trip was fabulous, the most powerful part was my off-road journey to the shamanic astrologer. A friend had highly recommended him and I was totally game. After getting wildly lost, with red dust pillowing in my rental's rearview mirror, I pulled up to a rickety old house that, hear me out, had *bars* on the windows. My intake of breath was audible. I checked my GPS three times and yep, I was in exactly the right spot. I walked down the steps toward his home with major trepidation, praying this wasn't a horrible mistake and I'd go missing, when a tall Asian man opened the door.

"My dear," he said. "Come right in. Don't worry, there is nothing to be afraid of."

He gestured to the interior of what appeared to be his home and opened the door wider. Fearful that he could already read my mind, I followed with my head down and my green juice gripped in my hand, at a slower, more hesitant pace than I usually walk.

The modest insides of his place didn't help the situation. He had a stained mattress on the floor with messy, light blue sheets scattered around it, a wall full – and I mean *full* – of books from floor to ceiling, and a card table surrounded by folding chairs so old and wobbly I wasn't sure they would be able to support me without cracking in half.

He grabbed my hands without any more of an introduction and opened the reading with a prayer. As bizarre as the circumstances were, I felt a wave of peace wash over me. I was suddenly willing to hear what this peculiar shamanic astro man had to say.

The reading went on forever; I swear I was there for over three hours. What someone could possibly say for three hours is beyond me, but it only felt like I was in that room with him for 30 minutes. What he said to me felt laughable at the time.

"Now listen to me when I say this," he said. "You are here for a tremendous mission and purpose. You are going to do big, big things. It's inevitable, truly. You will travel often, and you will become a renowned spiritual teacher in this lifetime." I spit my green juice out on the table at that one ... It was unfathomable to me in that moment. I was barely spiritual myself.

In fact, it felt like a fun, even silly adventure. Something I was doing because of where I was and the culture I was exploring. Little did I know he was planting a very important seed, almost a prophecy, that would lead me toward my own authentic power.

I was remembering that moment in 2013 when I had had my 4:59 "ten-minute" minute – my first quantum moment – and felt my whole body (and world) shake with desperation instead of reaching for my bottle of red. What had happened, I now realize, is that as fun-and-games as my meeting with the astrologer had seemed, I'd let his words sink into and stick with me. During my first quantum moment, I had started to pray for purpose (see page xxii).

That empowering whisper I'd heard telling me that there was so much more to life during that quantum moment wasn't just the universe but also a remembrance of the seed that shamanic astrologer had planted in 2011, which seemed to bubble back up to the surface. The words he had spoken had activated a curiosity inside me. It sent me on the path that led me to where I am today – in alignment with my soul, mentoring others and travelling the world to show people how to connect with and use their energy to manifest their dreams. He was right: that green juice should have made it down my throat instead of making a mess on his dusty card table. (By the way, I didn't break the folding chair, thank goodness!)

Another reflection I had flashed me back to a moment in 2012 in Austin, Texas. Remember, me and spas – we have a *thing*. A girlfriend of mine wanted a break from her littles and I'm almost always down for a fun adventure. We decided on a spa along the lake. This is where I first met my reiki (/reishi) healer (see page 18). Although I didn't realize it at the time, she would hold one of the keys on my journey to discovering my authentic power.

I didn't have my light-filled orgasm with her in 2012. She was disguised at the spa as a masseuse. She performed an intuitive massage on me (that was as fantastic as it sounds) and shared a very similar message to the one the shamanic astrologer had given me in Sedona. It felt curious, but it wasn't enough to awaken me yet.

Flash forward to 2013, when I decided to stop numbing, start feeling and finally shift my life for the better and she was on the forefront of my mind.

I was about to book a flight to Texas to try to find her when Sally suggested I try a search engine. Yes, the internet waves to the rescue again! With the hit of a button, her LinkedIn profile popped up. Happiness thrummed through me. Later, while chatting with her on the phone, she asked me a life-changing question:

"Suzanne," she said, "what would you be doing if you had no limits?"

"What do you mean by no limits? Of course, I have limits; we all do," I replied. I took in the deepest breath I had in as long as I could remember and out of nowhere it struck me: I was the one putting the limitations I thought I had on me. It was me that was limiting me. This realization set me free to pursue my dreams with renewed commitment.

When we step into alignment it's as if we are able to see things from a different perspective. When we can view the world from hindsight everything can change. In hindsight that trip to Sedona in 2011 was life-changing. Then again, the trip in 2012 where I thought I was simply adventuring and pampering myself was a key link to me connecting with my heart and my soul. And looking back, my dark night of the soul in 2013 actually catapulted me into my purpose, my passion and into living many of my dreams.

As a human species, we have only just begun to tap into the immeasurable possibilities available to us inside the quantum field. Just think of the advancements that have been made in the last decade. It's thrilling to think of the quantum leaps we will create when we add our hearts and our soulful superpowers to the game. I, myself, am only just getting started and I invite you to join me in jumping into the quantum field with your wonderfully aligned soul. You're bound to find magic there and your whole purpose for being.

Connect to the Quantum Field by Opening Up Your Heart and Mind

I invite you to take a moment now and think of a question that changed your life. What did it trigger? What did it spawn? Have you let it inspire you? If not, can you rehear it and heed the wisdom behind the inquiry now?

Then, consider this: if you had zero limits and could do anything, be anything and have anything, what would your life look like? Where would you be? How would you feel? How would it be different from what it is today? What does your heart want to show you?

Where in your life have seeds been planted that have stuck with you? How connected are you to your heart and soul – to that piece of divinity and perfection that lives right inside your heart?

If you walked into a mystical and magical button house today, what are the five buttons you would love to push? What dreams would they transport you to? How would your life look different if you followed these dreams with intent? Take a few minutes and really let yourself see each dream. Write down the details and maybe even share some of them with a trusted friend who will support your vision.

Still in your magical button house, now internalize what the possibilities that rest in the quantum field bring up for you, emotionally, viscerally, mentally and physically. Why? Because once you start to feel and experience what your ideal self and life could feel like, the closer you'll get to realizing your dreams.

QUANTUM TOOL #2
Connect to the Quantum Field
RECAP

Focus your energy on your dreams, align your personality with your heart and soul and pay more attention to infinite possibilities instead of all the reasons in front of you that make you think things aren't working – even if those limits are entirely within yourself. And a word of encouragement here: you've got this.

Your Blueprint for Positive Change

- Tune in to the quantum field by aligning your personality with your passions and discovering your soul's purpose.
- Understand that there is an infinite field of limitless possibilities that you can connect to at any time and any moment to begin to shift your reality.
- Play in the field of dreams and plug your energy into where you want to go, not what you believe is possible.
- The more expanded your energy is and the higher its vibration, the faster and easier you will create those big dreams.

3

Align with Love or Above

*"If you want to find the secrets of the universe,
think in terms of energy, frequency and vibration."*

Nikola Tesla

QUANTUM TOOL #3

Practise feeling more happiness and worthiness and allowing the good feelings in! Commit to treating yourself the way you would treat the person you love most. This could be with kind words, compassionate actions or simply a treat that will nourish your body, mind and spirit (just think of my awakening and how my love for luxe spas introduced me to my soul! (*See* page xxii.) When you fall away from love energy, rebound as quickly as possible by acknowledging your feelings with presence and compassion.

Enter the Jet Stream of Your Desires

In 2020 and 2021, I let more love into my life than I ever had before. True, I had had relationships in the past. Remember, too, that prior to my nightly happy hours and that radical lull in my life, I was certain my former boyfriend (the one I thought was my Prince Charming) and I would get married and live happily ever after. When that crumbled faster than a cookie in a toddler's hand, I closed off my heart. I completely forgot C S Lewis' words from *The Four Loves*: "The only place outside Heaven where you can be perfectly safe from all the dangers and perturbations of love is Hell." In other words? I began protecting myself from heartbreak by hardening myself. I put a shield over my heart because I was terrified of letting it break into pieces again. In the process of doing so, I started missing out on one of the primary reasons we are alive: love. Which, let me remind you, is the juicy target zone of the Hertz Vibration Scale (*see* page xxv).

I was ready, though. I had healed. I had turned up my vibes; I was oozing joy and appreciation around every corner. I had learned to tear down the walls that were guarding my heart, just as I had learned the power of accepting the unknown. In fact, I had learned how to *thrive* in the unknown.

It was in this energetic space that I met a man named Matt. He immediately felt like home. Our second date was so on point it seemed like I'd known him a decade, if not in another lifetime. He was and is handsome, athletic and masculine and has a heart of gold. He also possessed the most soothing presence of anyone I'd ever previously known. We laughed, we danced, we snuggled on the sofa and just had fun being together, no matter where we were.

But early on into our courtship (yes, I still use that word), Matt and I had a conversation. You know, *The* Conversation. We were incredibly compatible, we realized, but weren't totally a fit for a long-term relationship.

I felt crushed, even if it made sense on multiple levels. I genuinely thought I might have finally met my match. At that point in life, I understood the magnetism and power of leading with your heart. Of breathing deeply, being mindful, checking in with your emotions and allowing your intuition, rather than your logical mind, to run the show. And my intuition told me that, alas, he wasn't The One after all.

Although I knew it wasn't a forever-fit, that he was Mr Right Now and not my fairytale ending – every time I tuned into my heart, all I could hear was, *Enjoy it, anyway! Love him with all you've got.* That felt terrifying and completely against the "rules" many of us have been raised on, for finding your spouse or life partner. I threw caution to the wind and trusted my inner guidance system. I had faith in the voice I heard and my heart's true feelings.

It worked. I cherished every moment I had with Matt. He's a chef and made my Saturday morning ventures to the farmers' market even more special. He pampered me with five-star, romantic homemade dinners, which we relished, cozily. Everything felt like an escapade with him. Whether we were snorkelling, hiking, adventuring through a national park or just going to the grocery store, we had a ball. We always giggled and had a blast, no matter what. Our connection was fierce, palpable, passionate and playful. We were both very happy. We never argued, and I'm confident I have never been as present with anyone.

While it didn't last, I grew from that bond in numerous ways. It was my first time walking away from a relationship without feeling overwhelmed with bitterness or resentful or miserable – those feelings on the bottom rung on the vibration scale. Instead, I felt fulfilled and grateful for the experiences we had shared. It was if I walked away from him more aligned with and filled up with love energy than I ever had before.

Discovering A New Level of Self-love

As Matt and I were in the process of breaking up, I was hosting a leadership summit in Florida. I was trying to decide if I should invite Matt to join me. He was extremely supportive of my career and I knew he would be thrilled to be there. Unlike other momentous points in my previous relationships, when I looked to the outside to make decisions, this time I tuned into my heart. The voice that once told me to savour the connection I had with Matt now said those two words that are sometimes impossible to hear: *let go*. Only this time, I didn't feel an ache inside me from this wisdom. Freedom and appreciation bloomed instead.

Don't get me wrong. The logical part of me struggled with this because I had fallen for Matt. And yet I followed my intuition and my heart's voice and decided to head to Florida without him.

While all of my events are extraordinary, empowering and soul-expanding, this event had an extra flare of love energy. It was the first big event I had hosted since the unexpected halt that was placed on life in 2020 and all in-person contact and gatherings were suddenly nonexistent. The energy that moved through me on the stage was extraordinary, powerful, buoyant and magnificent.

Looking back, it's as if my connection with Matt allowed me to let more love in than I had realized possible. I adore my clients and the people who show up for my events. A continued theme I heard from them was, "Wow, you are truly glowing, Suzanne. Life is looking *great* on you." Such words pleased me and seemed entirely right because that's precisely how I felt. I remember having a moment of gratitude after the event because it was all just so perfect. So many breakthroughs, so much growth, massive levels of healing, and new soul friendships had transpired – no hiccups whatsoever! As I'm sure you can imagine, this is rare when you're hosting large events.

I was soaking in a bubble bath the evening after the event when I glanced down at my phone and saw Matt calling. It was terrific to hear his voice. What felt even better, though, was my trust in my decision not to invite him. If he had been there with me, I might have attributed the way I was feeling to him. Maybe I would have thought that having him there with me was what had created the glow my clients and attendees kept commenting on.

Although it would've felt wonderful to have him there, recognizing this new way of aligning to love or above was the most precious tool I could have ever received from Matt. I chose to love myself even more than him. I chose to honour my heart first and not care what anyone else would say or think. I chose me and, in doing so, I let even more love in.

We're taught to think that anything we want is outside of us, but searching like a hungry ghost and expecting others to make us happy inevitably leads to pain and disappointment. The love we desire is inside us. The question is, how can we align ourselves with others who can help lead us back to our own hearts?

When I reflect on 2020 and even 2021, my biggest lesson by far was amping up my love-or-above game. Again, love is the target zone, right underneath the ultimate tier of enlightenment. It comes in at 500 magical Hertz, its energy filled with momentum and limitless possibilities – and it's the vibe and literal key – to the quantum field.

Getting in Sync with Love or Above with Quantum Tool #3

The third Quantum Tool in my arsenal, **Align with Love or Above**, is all about riding upward in the energy jet stream, which is a powerful force that allows those possibilities the quantum field inspires to start materializing.

How? By consciously and consistently raising your vibration to "love or above," as Hawkins calls it (see the Hertz Vibration Scale, page xxv). This elevates our purpose and our energy to the highest frequencies of mindfulness. "Love is misunderstood to be an emotion; actually, it is a state of awareness, a way of being in the world, a way of seeing oneself and others," Hawkins states (and I couldn't agree more).

We are humans, flawed, certainly, but oh-so-capable once we start using our vibes to create the real life we crave. We are on a journey, evolving more today than we ever have before. We are being called to open up to a new and profound amount of love energy. To let it in, soak it up and give it back to others.

I want to be clear here. I am not suggesting that you force yourself into the love zone, that you use this lesson for self-serving purposes or you don't honour how you are truly feeling. In fact, when you witness the way you're feeling and you process it with compassion and empathy, you actually alchemize your vibration with love in that exact moment.

Read that again so it will sink in. **When you witness the way you are feeling and you honour it with compassion and empathy, you alchemize your vibration with love in that exact moment.**

What I am suggesting is this: accept the fact that you will move up and down this scale about eight million times. This doesn't matter; it's part of the human experience. What *does* matter is that you learn and hold onto the tools in this book to come back to the love zone as often as possible.

That day in 2013, that moment when I hit my knees and asked God for a positive way forward, I shifted on the Hertz Vibration Scale in an astounding way. I moved from the bottom, the red zone – from below zero, if you will – up to the green, the 300 Hz range because FINALLY, I was willing to choose a different path and to see a different way forward. There is no way we can get to the love zone if we aren't willing to select another route, while also accepting exactly where we are in the moment.

Vibing at love or above starts with loving yourself first, which is 100 per cent essential. I spent all those years dashing after a feeling that I wasn't even giving myself. I looked for love at the bottom of wine bottles, on dance floors and in relationships that weren't quite right for me and, worst of all, through the opinions of others. What I failed to do (and remember, failure is nothing if not an opportunity for change) was peer inside to see the bright light of my soul, and my pure positive power and inner strength.

If you want to create or manifest anything in your life, one of the most underutilized tools to do so is self-love, self-appreciation and self-compassion. This is what we should *really* be teaching in schools. This is what will transform your life. Your heart is the most magnetic force of creativity that you have. How are you treating it? Is it whole? Is it open?

The truth is your dreams are your responsibility and it's up to you to love yourself and get to know the real you so that your soul can shine and others can love you too.

A Dark Night of the Soul That Turned into Love

This is the first thing I shared with Sara, a client who had been referred to me by another client I had worked with for years. Sara reached out to me in the middle of her own dark night of the soul. A successful doctor who owned a private practice, she was suffering from the loss of the love of her life, who had recently walked away from the life they had built together. Her anxiety was off the charts. Her depression led her to dread waking up. She could hardly concentrate at work, and her work, obviously, was critical to others' wellbeing. The real kicker? Her son told her he no longer recognized her.

When I connected with Sara, I told her I could help her if she was willing to help herself. I explained that through my programme I would help her transform quickly, but she first had to accept where she was. I also added that if she was willing to take my advice and coaching, and implement the tools I gave her, magic would happen.

She agreed. It was quite miraculous, I must say, how swiftly she began to climb the vibration scale. I knew that all she needed was to come home to herself, again and again. To remember why she was living and exactly who she was living for.

I taught Sara about energy and the power of returning to her heart, just as I've taught you here. I asked her to put on a beginner's hat; to pretend like she didn't know anything about herself. Who was she, deep inside? What brought her pleasure? What brought her pain? What did she find fulfilling? What left her indifferent?

Sara shifted willingly and energetically. She opened her heart and began to heal layers of herself through our work together and through journal prompts, self-care practices and a strong-minded decision to be happy without falling into "toxic positivity" (forced "happiness" that can create more harm than good). So she let herself mourn the love of her life and stayed in those low "bye" vibes until she felt ready to alchemize them with love and ascend the vibration scale.

Just a few months into coaching, Sara would come to our calls with a smile on her face. Even across Zoom, she beamed with positive energy. She said she was falling in love with herself more and more, one day at a time. This had shifted and changed everything. Her private practice was flowing. Her son had rekindled his fondness for her and their relationship was more solid and joyful than it had ever been.

In time, Sara's ex came back. However, this time it was her choice to decide if it was what she wanted. She decided that it was and did so consciously. Thoughtfully.

Aligning with love or above isn't about getting an ex back, landing that dream job or even having the most glorious ocean view to wake up to every morning. Rather, it's about letting your birthright in. Opening up to receiving new levels of divinity in your human form.

This can feel unfeasible at first, especially if we don't believe we are worth it. But once we prioritize self-love and see how very valuable we are, we begin to feel lighter. Freer. More at ease with ourselves. Over time, this shifts to knowing that we are all here for a reason. That we are special and needed, in our own ways. This in turn leads to our full expression of self-love, and every morning feels like a gift.

I am on this path with you. I believe as long as we are breathing, we are growing and learning. I also believe there is always a next level. Today I can let more love in than I could last year. Hopefully, next year it will be even more. Sara was able to land in the love zone regularly (while previously living in the fear and shame zone) after only four or five months of intentionally deciding to align with love or above and by utilizing many of the tools in this book.

As I've mentioned previously, you are going to have bad days and you are going to have good days. This happens to the best of us, even if we tend to hover somewhere near the target 500Hz zone on the scale. When you can view yourself with sympathy and understanding for where you are, when you can value the low vibes you may be feeling, you automatically begin to transmute them with love.

Understanding vibration is one of the most transformational tools on your belt (or in your box, if that's more your thing). Nothing around you may or even can change – you have no, or limited, control over this. But if you change your energy and vibration, you can alter the *way* things around you unfold. People will meet you as you are, and if you're letting your light shine from a place of love or above, I assure you that magic will happen.

Say you walk into a party where others are complaining about their crappy day or their bulldog of a boss. You might feel unhappy because those vibes can drag you down to the bottom of the scale. You have a choice in this moment. You can calibrate down to their low vibes, or you can be sovereign in your love energy and hold a higher vibe – and thereby invite them to calibrate up to you. Energy is contagious and it's your choice who you spend time with and how powerful you can be with your vibes.

The magic is in holding the love-or-above energy in as many situations as possible. We live in a world that is dense sometimes, if not straight-up heavy, and if you can hold that energy of love, you will be become more magnetic than your wildest dreams. People will be drawn to you. They will want what you have. You will be the one people choose to sync up to and calibrate to so they can drop and alchemize their own low vibes.

High vibes say, "Get out of my way or rise up and join me." Allow me to reiterate it here: like attracts like. It really is that simple. It's the Law of Attraction – the irresistible, electrifying force of the universe that pulls together similar energies. I look to the Law of Attraction as a way to generate internal energy and lure in the circumstances I desire, no matter what is happening in the economy or the government; with my goals or personal life; on a global scale or even at the table next to me with all their gossip. The truth is, what will give you the most powerful quantum leap is when you can hold the love vibration when you are in the "in-between" state. Meaning, you've set your intention on a dream. You're turning up your vibration. You're giving your focus to where you want to go but it's just not here yet. THIS is when you anchor into the love energy and decide who you are going to be on the way to where you're going.

I used the Law of Attraction to flip my broken-down, old internal reality of attachments to ideas and beliefs that were no longer useful, healthy or serving me. And when I changed that internal energy, it changed me. That transformation allowed me to invite in and view new opportunities and insights I hadn't seen before – just as it let Sara feel happiness again, rebuild a bond with her son and have the choice (her *own* choice) whether or not to get back together with the love of her life whom she had thought she had lost forever.

Take this a step further and you'll find that love attracts love. Once you begin to align with love or above, you'll lure in what and who you love. Again, this all starts with how you love yourself and how you treat your own heart.

Your desires are placed in your heart from God, the Divine, the universe, according to your individual definition of a power beyond you. Your higher power gave these desires to you for a reason. Nurture yourself. Get to know the wisdom of your heart and soul. Shower yourself with aligned pleasure that feels good and exciting and serves your body in a positive way. Give yourself the space to be who you really are – and *bask* in it.

Align with Love and Above – Starting Today

When you look at the Hertz Vibration Scale (see page xxv), what comes up for you? Where do you spend most of your time? Are you in the lower vibrations of fear, grief and shame, or are you in the space of willingness and acceptance? How often do you land in the love zone?

What changes can you make, starting today, to let in more love? Can you say an empowered "yes" to exciting opportunities, and an equally empowered "no" to the people and things that no longer serve you? Can you simply accept where you are and be willing to choose another way or a different vibe or mindset? Where in your life do you need to view yourself with more empathy and compassion? How does your internal résumé read and what changes can you begin implementing to improve it?

QUANTUM TOOL #3
Align with Love or Above
RECAP

Practise feeling more happiness and worthiness and allowing the good feelings in! Commit to treating yourself the way you would treat the person you love most. This could be with kind words, compassionate actions or simply a treat that will nourish your body, mind and spirit (just think of my awakening and how my love for luxe spas introduced me to my soul! (*See* page xxii.) When you fall away from love energy, rebound as quickly as possible by comforting your feelings with presence and compassion.

Your Blueprint for Positive Change

- Give yourself full permission to let more love in. Allow yourself to receive more romantic love, more family love, more friendship love and even more love through your colleagues and profession.
- If your vibrations fall from the zone or feeling of love and above, treat yourself with compassion and grace so that you can rebound as quickly as possible.
- Allow yourself to experience the way emotions make you feel and then alchemize your lower vibrations with love.
- It's up to you how powerfully you influence your surroundings and the people you meet with your vibes.

4

Reprogram and Rewire
Your Mind

*"It's time to be defined by a vision of the future
instead of memories of the past."*

Dr Joe Dispenza

QUANTUM TOOL #4

Understand the way your mind works. When things are not
working for you, go within and look at the stories you have
and are aligning with in your mind. Take your power back and
begin to tell a new story. Create a fresh narrative that will
take you where you want to go, making sure that it's exciting
and imaginative and everything you've ever dreamed of. It is,
after all, where you're meant to be.

Genie in a Bottle

Have you ever wished you had a genie in a bottle that could grant you wishes on command? I've loved the idea of three wishes ever since I saw *Aladdin* as a little girl. (Of course, my first wish has always been for *unlimited* wishes!)

Wishing is a large part of getting your quantum vibe on, but by the end of this programme you'll know that wishing is just the *start* of the whole process.

Why? Because wishing is attached to the notion that it'll never happen. "I wish," after all, is totally distinct from "I will." (In fact, changing your language to "I will" can shoot you up the Hertz Vibration Scale – and rapidly at that.)

My method, the one you're learning all about here, is about shifting your vibration to the scale's highest realms and taking a quantum leap so that you can realize your biggest, most dazzling dreams.

So, we've already dug into energy and vibrations. We've covered the Law of Attraction and understand that like attracts like.

Now it's time to talk about perhaps the most powerful tool of all, which shapes just how high your vibes can rise: understanding the way your brain works and how to get your subconscious mind to work *for* you and not against you.

The conscious part of your mind – I'm sure you know – is the part you're aware of. But what do you think *sub*conscious means? If conscious means "aware of", then "subconscious", in bare-bones terms, means "unaware."

Studies performed by neuroscientists at institutions ranging from Stanford to MIT show that the subconscious mind is running the show in our lives approximately *90* per cent of the time.

Let me repeat that: **your subconscious mind is in the driver's seat *85–90 per cent of the time.***

I was shocked when I first heard this. Downright baffled, even, to the point that I was like, *Say what? The part of me I am unaware of is essentially dominating my life?* What do you mean, *subconscious* mind? How do we have something that is such a huge part of us and we're not even, well, *conscious* of it?

But it's true. Whatever you're doing right now (besides reading or listening to this book) is due to your subconscious. Chewing, walking, running the dishwasher, adding organic gummy bears to your Instacart – all are happening because of a discreet navigational device that doesn't even tell you it's *on*. (And, it's almost always going …)

The implications of this are tremendous, of course. Primarily, this means that our lives are set on autopilot, because our minds are responding to the habits we've established and the instructions we've given them. How many times have you hopped in your car to go to work, the grocery store or yoga? You jump in the car, crank the ignition and are well on your way. Before you have another conscious thought, you're in the parking lot of your destination. You checked out and went to another place in your mind but somehow still ended up in the precise spot you wanted to reach.

Equipped with this knowledge of just how powerful our subconscious is, I set myself a mission to understand as much about it as I could. I was determined to learn how to utilize this aspect of me to work – and work *well* – for me.

Part of my research included getting cozy and acquainted with our different brain waves. What does this mean? Think of it like this: brain waves are electrical impulses that are activated by our neurons. Basically, they are info go-betweens that, through those impulses and chemicals, send "data" between different regions of the brain *and* the nervous system. The cool thing? Brain waves happen at different frequencies and define our emotions, thoughts, behaviours, levels of concentration and more.

Here's the breakdown of these brain waves for you:

- Delta
- Theta
- Alpha
- Beta
- Gamma

Now, no need to memorize these – trust that I don't give out report cards on this process – but the one I want to focus on here is theta. (Quick side note, though: remember the reiki and energy healing I did and continue to do? It activates alpha brain waves, which are slower brain waves that, in essence, move you into idle. In this state, you're chilled and peaceful, which is why I usually describe reiki as a ray of light.)

Theta brain waves are the ticket to quantum moments, expansion and becoming a super-attractor of your dreams. Suffice to say, for now, that once you've tapped into this magical place, you feel dreamy and sleepy, maybe even spacey (albeit in a *good* way). It's that airy, lovely place between wakefulness and slumber.

Now, back to our subconscious: as I've said, our minds respond to the habits we've established, but they also react to the orders we give and the "noise" we allow to enter.

This last bit is *uber-important*, as it's safe to say that the majority of us, if not all, have let toxicity absorb into our minds, bodies and energy from the hours of news and other media (particularly during the pandemic) we consume and the social media we scroll through daily.

Every single day, we're programming our mind and our energy. Mainstream media, Instagram, TikTok, Facebook and millions of marketing firms understand this all too well – just think of the film, *The Social Dilemma*. Media and marketers are masterminds at pushing our buttons and triggering both our desires and fears. They know the language to speak to us in and do this in a way that their messages drop right into the part of our brain governing our lives and making decisions. Have you ever thought you had an illness simply because you saw a commercial for treatments for it – oh, only like 100 times? Have you ever noticed how swiftly you believe what news anchors are saying without ever questioning if it's actually true? Have you ever been overwhelmed by the compulsion to buy that bracelet or hat on Instagram because it just looks so *you*?

Our subconscious minds soak up what they're exposed to – and this goes beyond the realm of media, social or otherwise. As children, we assume thought patterns, perceptions and opinions based on three main things: our surroundings; what our parents, society and those closest to us tell us; and the "beliefs" we begin to think about ourselves.

Such – often well-meaning – influences can calibrate us to believe we are undeserving. Things said to us as kids, such as "Shut up!" "Who do you think you are?" and "You will never amount to anything," become the soundtrack running, sometimes silently (or oh-so-subtly) in our brains and bodies. Indeed, when we hear such words, especially from someone we love or respect, they can stick with us to the point that they become integrated into our subconscious minds, thereby encoding us with feelings of unworthiness. (To this day, one of my friends wears close-toed shoes if she's gone more than two weeks without a pedicure. If not, all she hears, on repeat, is her mother condemning her for her chipped nail polish.)

A Billionaire's Mindset

As adults, we run programs and thought loops inside our mind that are based on the internal judgements and views that we soaked up as kids. For example, I have a client named Tim who is crazy-successful and self-made. He always leads with his heart, owns five companies and all are cosmically *thriving.* When we looked at his patterns together, we realized that one of the things that made him so successful is that at a very young age he believed and was afraid he wouldn't live past the age of 50. (This is because he had suffered a great deal of loss and grief when he was a child.) This specific story served him well in his career because, where many people put things off and procrastinate, his mindset was *I'd better do it now because I might not have tomorrow.*

Tim achieved happiness, fulfillment, a loving family and an awesome circle of friends – all by the age of 45. (Not to mention a level of wealth that would blow your mind.) In his case, his subconscious *helped* him create a rich and rewarding life. The best part? He's still striving to reach the next higher plane, both professionally and personally.

Change Your Beliefs and Change Your Life

I have seen those who take on crippling stories, too. Money is bad, they think, or money doesn't grow on trees. Or they believe that having wealth is selfish and corrupt – all because that's what they heard growing up. They've been programmed to believe that money isn't available. It's imprinted in their mind and therefore their energy field. It goes without saying that this belief totally shapes how they move through life and their tier of success and abundance.

Conventional belief suggests that in order to change or reprogram, you must get to the root of your story or program. I disagree. I don't believe you have to understand exactly where your programming was derived from or when. Sure, there are certainly times and cases where it can be helpful to explore this; talk therapy can be beneficial – why else would it have been used as a therapeutic technique since Freud? But I also believe even more that the energy and frequency of where we are today, right now, is supremely important. This might be a controversial opinion in the personal development world, but it's what I feel intuitively and where I believe we, as humans, are now. The veil to access higher level frequencies and to open the door to the subconscious mind is thin and we can quantum leap into a place where we're healed and whole when we tap into the right energy and vibration. Creating an awareness of old habits and rewiring our energy to align with where we want to go isn't just effective, it's powerful and life-changing. I'm not claiming it's a one-size-fits-all. But I am saying that we have faster ways of healing and transforming available to us today than we have ever had before.

When pondering these stories, experiences and programs that guide your subconscious, you might see, right away, where your limiting belief and old story came from. This can serve you well. If it's clear where the story came from, then spend some time with that. Let yourself awaken to the fact that this story is a coding that you took on and not actual truth. (More of this is covered in the exercise in the Workbook, see page 157.)

Other times, however, it may not work in your favour to dig up traumatic memories. It might be in your best interest to merely honour where you are on your journey today, sort out what arises and boldly look at these stories with acceptance, love and a willingness to allow them to move through you. As you notice a feeling, you can start to tune into why you are feeling this way. The journal prompts on pages 188–189 can help you uncover the reasons. Sometimes it's more powerful to focus on the now and where we desire to go rather than giving so much power to the past.

As you allow your feelings and emotions to roll through you from a compassionate place, you'll begin to alchemize these tales with love, the target zone. In doing so, you'll give yourself the opportunity of a clean slate and a fresh start. From here, you'll be able to write a new story – one that'll fire you up and fuel your dreams.

I had a powerful breakthrough on all of this when I read Harry Carpenter's *The Genie Within*. This book suggests thinking of your subconscious mind like a genie in a lamp. The thoughts you think and the questions you ask tell your genie what you would like.

Case in point: if you ask yourself questions like, *Why doesn't anything ever work out for me? Why is this happening to me? Ugh, just as I thought, this went terribly*, then you're effectively asking your subconscious genie to find negative answers to these downbeat questions.

It's your job to intentionally ask questions that will serve your dreams and desires. So what if you frame the questions differently by asking, *Where is the opportunity here? What are my next steps to facilitate a much better outcome? How can this experience translate into more joy and abundance?* Well, your subconscious – yep, that thing you're not even aware of – will work tirelessly to supply you with answers. So, if you change the song and tune into a higher frequency, where willingness, acceptance, reason, love and pleasure predominate, you will be vibing at the level on the scale where you can realize those dreams and fulfill those desires.

Resetting Your Mind with Quantum Tool #4

In my fourth Quantum Tool, **Reprogram and Rewire Your Mind,** I am giving you a road map of how to unleash your own inner genie in a bottle! (And yes, you get more than three wishes!)

The first thing we need to do is understand, exactly, what I've explained above.

Recall what I said about driving? About how you can jump into your car and, without really being aware of it, arrive where you set out to go? Over the years, I have asked this question to thousands of people. Every time, when I speak at events, nearly every person in the audience nods and raises their hand, recognizing that this has happened to them – and happens on a regular basis. I'm guessing it's happened to you at some point as well. Your subconscious mind took over because you programmed it to get you to where you wanted to go.

This translates into other spheres of life. The first thing I did when I learned about the subconscious mind? I started taking an inventory of what I was letting into my life daily. Was I listening to toxic news or watching detrimental things on TV, without really realizing it? Nope, I had stopped doing that in my late 20s. I noticed I didn't feel good when I listened to the news and the solution was simple: turn it off. I used to go to bed with my TV on; now, my entire body cringes at the thought of it. In my "Girl Awakened" state – as I am now – I listen to binaural beats or a meditation, or work toward deliberately reprogramming my subconscious mind with affirmations and thoughts that are aligned with my dreams so they will continue while I'm sleeping. Why? Because even when we're out cold, our subconscious mind is awake. In fact, this is an excellent time to utilize what I like to call intentional reprogramming.

After I was already deep into rewiring and reprogramming my subconscious mind, and helping many of my clients do the same, I found the work of Dr Joe Dispenza, who says – and I'm paraphrasing here – what separates the conscious and subconscious mind is the analytical mind. Your subconscious mind operates on a programme of habits, behaviours and emotions, all of which are tied to memories and the past. This is the genius of meditation. It's a tool that teaches people how to change their brain waves – how to slow them down; to reach that theta state (see page 62). When you begin to slow your brain waves, you begin to have access to the space inside your mind where you can reprogram your subconscious mind and create enduring change.

Knowledge is for the mind. Experience is for the body. In that moment of experience, you are embodying knowledge and wisdom. It is literally in your cells, creating magnetism in your body.

Once I heard Dr Joe explain it like this, I realized how fantastically powerful meditation is when it comes not just to shutting down the endless chatter of the "monkey mind" but also to reprogramming and *rewiring* your mind.

In each meditation, you're teaching your body emotionally to feel the outcomes of what you desire. The feelings of your big, wild dreams are stamped into your cells. You're essentially rehearsing your success over and over in your mind's eye (just think of professional athletes and musicians who call upon visualization for drive – something we'll get into later). On the way, you're rewiring and reprogramming your subconscious mind, as well as becoming a vibrational match to where you consciously want to go. This is a chance to generate a new story in your mind, body and soul, to deliberately create with your biggest superpower, your very own energy.

Let me explain how this is possible. As I touched upon above, we have electrical impulses occurring in our brain that create waves or bands. As I also said, I want to help you understand theta brain waves, which are linked to creativity, daydreaming and peace. When you're in a theta state, you're in a place where you're just barely aware – and it is here that the door to the subconscious mind is wide, wide open.

With this door wide open, you can rewrite the script. According to Dr Joe, you can literally change the genetics and coding of your cells and DNA by syncing your body with calculated higher-vibe energy and uplifting thoughts. The theta state helps you enter the subconscious mind, which creates a door straight into the quantum field. Remember that the universe speaks in energetics and emotions. Honing in on these tools will help you arrive there at turbo speed. You navigate your mind and body to be able to access it, and once you're there, you look beyond your human aspects. There is no logic or meaning in the quantum field. It is the key to steering yourself free from the limitations you put on yourself.

And there's a fabulous bonus with this relaxed state: theta will help override your subconscious mind, which, as we all know, can sometimes be vicious. Just think of that poisonous media and negative self-talk it has absorbed and those bad habits and limiting beliefs you have carried around that didn't even originate with you.

You can reach theta in meditation and other hypnotic states, and you achieve theta brain waves when you're lightly sleeping or dreaming but not quite in the deepest phases of slumber. You know that moment, first thing in the morning, when you stretch, take a breath and feel like you're floating as you slowly open your eyes? That is theta.

Or, you know when you're lost in the tasks that you're performing or the project you're creating; when you lose track of time and are just connected and present? (Also known as "in the flow" or "in the zone.") This too is theta. Or that feeling when your mind is on the brink of shutting off – that cerebral slip – right before you fall asleep? Theta again – and it's spectacular.

Many meditations and sounds can take you into theta. Those binaural beats I mentioned earlier? They work beautifully. Crystal sound and Tibetan healing bowls are just a few other sounds that can shift you into this dreamy place.

The benefits of striking this brain wave are copious. Numerous studies have demonstrated that it's the ideal brain wave state to be in for mind and body healing, in part because theta promotes profound levels of relaxation. This band in your brain can also boost your immune system, reduce your stress and anxiety, which, let's face it, we *all* need during these days, and enhance your creativity and intuition. It's also, again, the perfect sweet spot to be in to reprogram your subconscious.

Dr Rick Hanson, who is the author of *Hardwiring Happiness* and *Buddha's Brain* among other titles, confirms this. "Mindfulness meditation ..." he says, "is characterized by an open presence and a non-judgemental awareness of sensory, cognitive and affective experiences as they arise in the present moment. The handful of research studies examining EEG activity" – a test that examines abnormalities in your brain waves – "during mindfulness meditation practice consistently reports increases in frontal theta power as well as increased frontal theta communication."

"This is important," he goes on to write, "because theta is a slow brain wave and may serve as a counterbalance to the typical fast brain wave activity observed in persons experiencing chronic stress and anxiety."

Translation? Landing in the theta playground quiets the mind, thus allowing you to enter a state in which you *feel* the results of realizing your dreams.

This isn't to say that meditation is as simple as sitting in the lotus position, closing your eyes and falling into that marvellous theta state. Trust me on this. I dabbled with meditation at first, and that's putting it lightly. When I closed my eyes, all I could see and hear were the thousand thoughts I was thinking and the gazillion things I needed to do. It made me jumpy, which confused me further. Wasn't this supposed to be soothing? I felt like ants were crawling out of my skin.

I also thought I wasn't doing it right and, if you know me by now, I'm sure you can see that I'm someone who likes to excel at everything I endeavour. *This isn't working,* I told myself over and over again, and kept opening my eyes and looking around the room and wondering what I should have for lunch and if *for sure* I had unplugged my hair wand and should I buy that other pair of pants I like and, my gosh, *did* I pay that bill? And so on and so forth. My mind was, frankly, too busy because I was so busy being busy. Plus, what was I supposed to be feeling? *This?* Really? Nah, a bottle of Pinot was far more effective and honestly much easier.

I stayed with it, though. Like anything in life, if you want success, you keep going. You build up to your goal. No one expects to go to the gym once and have six-pack abs or scroll-worthy biceps by the next morning. It's the same with rewiring your mind. It's a practice; something you continually cultivate. Now, I can say, in all sincerity, that I have meditated every single day since 11 May, 2014! I haven't missed a single day since then. I don't do it because I'm hyper-disciplined, either. I do it because I understand the power I'm creating through this daily practice. It expands my heart, opens up my connection to the quantum field, turns up my vibes – and is a fabulous catalyst for the persistent reprogramming of my mind.

I started by listening to guided meditations and found them extremely helpful. Then I began creating guided meditations at my events and for my clients because I knew how transformative this practice could be. (I have several guided meditations for you in the Workbook. If you'd like audio meditations, you can get a few free ones at www.suzanneadamsinc.com).

Reconditioning Your Beliefs to Create a New Story

I had a client named Jack who had a terrific desire to create success inside his online coaching business. He came to me committed and ready for a breakthrough.

Jack had had his own business for about two years and had reached a few milestones here and there, but he just couldn't seem to make more money than roughly $2,000 (£1,500) a month. He knew his purpose and that his calling was to reach many and he didn't understand why he was stuck – and had been for a while.

He joined one of my coaching programmes and began to rewire and reprogram his mind and energy.

He was an A-plus student. He showed up with an open heart to every training and coaching call inside the programme.

Very quickly, something clicked inside Jack. He did the inner work and the rewiring techniques I shared with him. (Many of them are in the Workbook in Part 2.) Jack became unbridled in his authentic power. He began oozing much more love energy than he ever had before. He was shifting the neurons in his cells and brain, which prepped him for success. Jack began to double his monthly sales and then, two months later, he tripled them. Within six months, he was consistently making $18,000 (£13,500) to $20,000 (£15,000) per month. What's more? He was reaching and serving *ten times* the number of people he had before.

None of this, of course, is necessarily about money. Although I believe money is a powerful resource that magnifies the energy you already carry, it's just one sign of how effective vibing up can be. Jack followed the process I am sharing with you and he shifted his business and lifestyle. Heart-centred, indeed.

Quantum Leaping into Success

I have another client, Monique, who had a partnership in an engineering firm. Monique is one of the most amazing women I know. She has been a long-term client and I have had the privilege and pleasure of watching her grow, expand and continue to use these Quantum Tools. She went from being a partner in a company to having the desire to be the first woman to own a company in her industry. She didn't know how she was going to do it and she almost didn't believe she could. I helped her see new possibilities and showed her how to shift her energy and use her power to anchor into the quantum field. Monique had some old programming to work through and together we were able to rewire and reprogram her mind to align with her bravest, biggest dreams.

Monique ultimately started her own company and although she launched it just before the start of the pandemic and therefore had some unexpected hurdles to overcome, she had the tools to understand how to manifest optimistically with her energy. She was able and willing to "sit in the fire" with new stories that emerged and were not in alignment with her revitalized vision. Monique is such a delight to coach because her energy is so receptive and she is able to rewire and reprogram very quickly! She's now thriving in her new company; in fact, she did three million dollars (£2.25 million) in sales this year and just sent out her very first million-dollar proposal.

Writing this now brings tears to my eyes because in addition to creating a dream she once believed was impossible, she has also learned to love herself, has taught her daughter to do the same and has a deeper and more passionate relationship with her husband than ever. She wrote to me recently thanking me and telling me what an important part I have had in her continued transformation.

The truth is, I am simply a guide for her; a vessel to help her recalibrate her energy, to upgrade her mindset and to own a new level of empowerment. Monique understands the power of repetition and continuing to stay on the path of using these tools and allowing herself to evolve and grow with each iteration as she follows this process. And now? It's your turn.

So, ready for that game plan? Jump right in.

Rewire and Reprogram Your Mind

Step 1: Take inventory of what you're allowing into your energy and your mind.

What people, circumstances, literature, films or media are you consuming that's not working to your advantage? Which of these things are turning your vibes down instead of up?

Become conscious of what you need to shift so you *can* shift it. Do you need to be in more spaces and places with high-vibe content and conversations? Do you need like-minded people in your circle cheering you on instead of telling you "to be realistic" or that your dreams are impossible? Be truthful with yourself. Act accordingly, and do so promptly.

Step 2: Understand how quickly meditation can help you rewire your brain and drop you into the theta waves state.

When you comprehend that you can shift your brain waves into a theta state, you become impressionable and can rewrite the script of your life and weave the gorgeous, joyful web that you envision. Meditation is a highly valuable way to rewire your subconscious mind into alignment with your heart, soul and dreams.

Every time something isn't going your way, there's a solid chance it's because you are either vibing way down on the Hertz scale or because you have a hidden belief stuck in your subconscious that you picked up somewhere along the way – most likely in your childhood.

The art of amplifying your genie is to get up close and personal with how you're feeling – a theme, as I'm sure you can see by now, that is a large part of my programme and process. Meditation helps with this as well. Many of us are too "busy" to sit with our feelings. Have you ever been busy being busy? I'm going to take a wild guess and say that you have. A packed social calendar, never-ending meetings, to-do lists at work, errands. Soccer games, baseball practices, ballet pick-ups, laundry, cooking, blowouts for date nights and live concerts, trips to the grocery store, the gym – the list goes on and on. It's endless. And while lots of life is pleasurable, being too busy being busy can keep you from entering a theta state and altering your subconscious.

In the process of opening and healing my heart, I began to check in with how I was feeling: Every Single Day. Back in 2013, when I had my awakening, I decided to dedicate the entire year of 2014 to learning to love myself. How could I expect others to love me if I didn't even love myself? One of the things I had to learn was to get intimate with myself and my heart. That began with identifying how I was feeling and learning what things would bring this new awakened version of me bliss. I had to reacquaint myself with well, myself. Who was I, anyway? Who was this soul inside? It may sound silly, but it was a powerful part of my reprogramming and rewiring.

When we get quiet and still with our feelings, we create emotional intelligence. If we don't know how we're feeling, how in the world can we make changes? If we aren't aware of the programs we're running, how can we turn the dial to a new tune? The human default is to numb. Numb with alcohol or Netflix; or scrolling through five different social feeds; or spending four hours online shopping; or binging on cupcakes or milkshakes; or cleaning until your hands are red. Or being busy being busy!

With this in mind, ask yourself: what is my numbing method of choice? Can I bring it into my awareness and conscious mind, starting now? Can I shift it toward healing? Can I be silent and stationary with my emotions and feel them and allow them to pass through me? What is my part in shifting these vibes so I can get higher on the scale?

Step 3: Get out of survival and into love.

You know what survival feels like. It's the three big Fs: fight, flight or freeze. These responses happen in your nervous system in response to any sort of stimuli that feels threatening, whether it's your boss yelling at you or an argument with your significant other or even someone sketchy walking down the street.

The problem is this: these bodily reactions evolved eons ago when humans really did encounter tigers and had to choose between these three Fs in order to survive. We haven't outgrown these knee-jerk responses so, once we sense alarm, and if our nervous systems aren't trained, we can fall right back into them.

In short, it's not a fun way to live if you're stuck in survival mode. Unfortunately, many of us are – and without even being aware of it. When we're trapped in fight mode, we react from a place of disconnection, and it's almost impossible to reach those supernova theta waves from this place.

So, start to notice the moments you feel unsafe, as well as the times in which you're reactive and not making decisions from a grounded place of love. You have the power inside you to train your autonomic nervous system into love and out of stress, and away from these three Fs. I spent many – too many – years searching and thinking everything I needed was outside of me. The truth is it was in my heart all along. You will not get the reprogram and upgrade from outside of you. It simply doesn't exist there. It lives *in you*. It's right inside your heart, which you will be able to feel more and more as you experience that theta state we discussed – and also by tapping into the energy of appreciation.

Studies show that when you practise gratitude every day for a month, you create a habit. And when we create a habit, we change the way the neurons in our brain fire, which can be into more positive, automatic thinking and behaviours. The more we practise gratitude, the stronger this rewiring becomes. When we think more positively, we emit a higher-vibe frequency and therefore begin magnetizing our dreams with our energy.

To take this a step further, when you can ignore what is happening around you and dive into the feeling of what you desire, you're training your mind to align with and create the very reality you're plugged into and *not* the reality that other sources are trying to show you and program for you.

A beautiful thing about our mind, including our subconscious mind, is that it can't tell the difference between what is real and what is imagined. A study conducted at Harvard Medical School, by a man named Alvaro Pascual-Leone, ascertained just this.

Pascual-Leone was initially studying how much of the motor cortex of the brain controlled finger movement in piano players. The first group in the study practised a five-finger piano exercise every day for five days. The second group was told to visualize the same finger exercise in their minds, imagining moving their fingers. They also practised in their minds the same amount of time as the other group did on actual pianos.

He had an unusual second finding at the end of the study, in that it displayed a groundbreaking aspect of the brain – the capacity of sheer thought can alter its structure and grey matter. This meant that the part of the brain regulating the fingers and movements of those playing the piano also enlarged in the brains of those who *visualized* playing on the ivory keys.

"Mental practice resulted in a similar reorganization of the brain," Pascual-Leone later wrote. What is the implication for you and me, for all of us? It means that mentally practising anything – from vinyasa to football to, hey, even kissing, can result in superiority without the physical practice. Moreover? Mental training or visualizing can alter the structure of your brain. When you visualize and imagine something vividly, you are training your brain to change its biochemistry and create an actual memory.

Let me repeat that.

Simply by visualizing and imagining, you are rewiring and reprogramming neurons in your brain. Your imagination can alter your neurons. You can attune the energy and cells in your body to what you desire to create through adjusting your energy to it, merely with the tool of visualization. It's proven – and it's potent.

If a belief is merely a thought we think over and over again, our thoughts create our reality. But what if we bend our thoughts to correspond with a reality we actually want and think them over and over again to imprint new beliefs into our physical being? You can choose to create a different story starting NOW. If that doesn't get you excited and help you feel empowered, I don't know what will!

Remember, the questions you ask yourself determine your reality. What are three questions you remember asking yourself recently? What are three questions you are committed to asking yourself moving forward?

QUANTUM TOOL #4
Reprogram and Rewire Your Mind
RECAP

Understand the way your mind works. When things are not working for you, go within and look at the stories you have and are aligning with in your mind. Take your power back and begin to tell a new story. Create a fresh narrative that will take you where you want to go, making sure that it's exciting and imaginative and everything you've ever dreamed of. It is, after all, where you're meant to be.

Your Blueprint for Positive Change

- Understand how to let your subconscious work on your behalf.
- Creating an awareness of old habits and rewiring your energy to align with where you want to go is powerful and life-changing.
- Relaxing into theta brain waves is a gateway into the door to the subconscious and your ticket to quantum vibes.
- Simply by visualizing and imagining, you are rewiring and reprogramming neurons in your brain and shifting your reality.

5

Repurpose Your Energy

"Choose courage over comfortability."
Brené Brown

QUANTUM TOOL #5

Let yourself feel your "low vibes" and utilize that energy to inspire a new solution you would never have thought of otherwise to find motivation, and to spur you into the quantum field. Give yourself permission to express yourself and claim your worth. As well as a downside, triggers have an upside – and an awesome one at that.

Turn Your Triggers Into Gold

Can you guess what two words in the English language are the biggest blockades in the way of you and your dreams? Yep, you guessed it. In my opinion, the words "I know" can construct a monumental wall in your energy, which thwarts many, if not all, manifestations.

"No one can afford me," and "I'm stuck here," my friend Jill – a woman I had known and whose company I had enjoyed immensely – said feeling deflated and annoyed, a few years ago. Jill was an all-round badass and Executive Vice President at one of the most successful athleisure companies, not only in the United States but also across the globe. I love Jill and admire the heck out of her too, but there were times when I was annoyed with her as well. She had an "I know" attitude and could be totally resistant to change, which was completely opposite to my MO (*modus operandi*).

When we think we know everything – and know it best – we aren't exactly open and connected to the quantum field. In fact, we're closing ourselves off to it, as the quantum field operates on the notion that anything is possible. Remember, it's a place where imagination rules – and our imaginations are nothing if not an exploration of what we *don't* know.

Jill wasn't wholly down for the concept of the quantum field because she couldn't see it as something palpable; again, she had that "I know" perspective that was not only exasperating me but also wreaking havoc in her life. And so, I used a long-term approach. She wasn't willing to see things differently which meant that until she was ready for a fresh angle, I wasn't going to be able to help her.

Meanwhile, Jill watched in the background as I helped top executives create breakthroughs, purpose, abundance and increased happiness. I assisted others with landing their dream, heart-centred careers (those that are aligned with their purpose and mission). I helped many more realize such "high-vibe" energy that they attained precisely what they desired, whether that was manifesting a dream or greater physical health. I helped others still crank up their self-confidence and become connected with their purpose, which naturally translated to them finding their whole reason for being alive.

In response? Jill's respect for me grew.

Jill began to ask for my guidance. She craved something new; she wanted more. She had been with her company for 15 years and was put off by the way she was treated during the pandemic. She had taken over a brand that was down 50 per cent in sales, although under her particular leadership, it was down only 14 per cent. (This is impressive under any circumstances, but especially when the entire world is shaken to its core.) Jill's bonus was taken away from her and her boss told her she wasn't impressed with what she had done.

Jill was affronted. She was angry about the 50 per cent cut in her income, sure, but she was even more fired up that she had been working 12- to16-hour days, managing all of the major global time zones – China, Europe, the US

– which had left her, naturally, slaving away at odd hours. She didn't receive so much as a simple "good job," not even a "thank you."

You may be thinking, *Well, I would be angry too!* Rightfully so. But anger can be a debilitating thing – unless we manipulate it to our advantage.

Here's the thing about the energy of anger. Although it's not at the top of the Hertz Vibration Scale, it has the incredible potential to generate movement, motivation, momentum and change. Have you ever been broken up with, felt both heartbroken and miffed, mourned your ex for a bit – and then decided to make a major, positive overhaul of your life, whether it was finally going for that cute bob you were after, changing your style to your own liking (and not your partner's), pursuing that dream job in a city that they said they'd *never* move to or spending time with those friends you had sorely missed? That's exploiting the hot, agitated energy you feel when you're angry in a *good* way. It's a trigger that's triggering more than "low vibes." It's triggering constructive, fabulous change. It's anger working in your favour because you know how to whip it into something wonderful.

Anger inspired Jill. She was no longer willing to sit by and watch as she was blatantly disrespected by the company she'd been devoted to for years. With my input, she began to open up her consciousness to the idea that other, even better opportunities were well within her reach.

Jill lived on the US coast in an area she had come to love so much that she didn't want to move. She originally feared there wouldn't be a job opportunity in her region, at least not one that could compare with or exceed her current position and the salary that came with it (even if it had dipped). Jill explained that what she really wanted was respect, kindness, fairness, appreciation. She loosened her "I know" stance and saw the possibilities of the quantum field. Then, she began to play with it (or, rather, *in* it) and grasped what her life could look like if she truly was limitless.

In doing so, she became magnetic. She couldn't believe all of the opportunities that started falling into her lap.

Jill was approached by a new, celebrity-based brand that was preparing to launch. A few other, smaller companies reached out and expressed their desire not only to hire her but also to compensate her in alignment with what she was already making, *plus more*.

Despite Jill's anger and resentment, she felt loyal to her company – after 15 years, how could she not? She genuinely didn't want to leave; she just wanted what she knew she deserved. She also needed to honour her feelings and do what was best, not just for her company but also for *herself*.

After sifting through all of the prospects that had "fallen into her lap" (that's code for a progressive shift in energy), she recognized they were happening because *she* was operating on a whole new level. She was letting more love in. She was reprogramming and rewiring her mind to new possibilities. She had repurposed her "low vibe" anger to work on her behalf – and she became irresistible as a result.

Jill narrowed down her offers and opportunities to three of her top choices, which we discussed. She couldn't quite decide and, in our consultation, I noticed she was restricting herself. She began to look at what her logical mind thought was likely, not what her heart sincerely desired. I guided Jill to a place of new possibility and connection, and asked her to make a list of everything she desired from that space, not what she believed was feasible.

Jill did exactly that and obtained the clarity she needed. She decided her best option was to take the offer with the number one competitor of her current company. She messaged me with what they presented to her and, while I felt her enthusiasm, I could see there was still so much left on the table. I coached her back to that place of anger (she is, after all, a friend and I know how to push her buttons) and had her utilize that anger energy once again to courageously request what she knew she was worth. After two weeks of negotiations, she had a great result.

"You are not going to believe what they offered me!" she said when she called after two weeks of negotiations. Jill had gotten every single thing she had asked for and more. Now, came the hard part – facing her colleagues and work family from the last decade and a half and letting them know she would be saying *ciao*.

I was thrilled for her. I knew her work ethic, her talent, her value. But I could also feel that this entire enterprise, and her decision surrounding it, wasn't over yet.

"Jill, I know this may not make logical sense at first," I said, "but you are not going to be working for this new company. I can feel it in my bones."

"I know it seems like such a big move, but yes, I am," she replied, that "I know" tone returning. "I'm giving my notice today."

Even though Jill was convinced she was sure, I sensed it wasn't over. Typically, in Jill's industry, you get a single chance to walk away and they'll give you a counter-offer once. Should you refuse it, they let you go. She had already tried to resign roughly five years earlier. The company was very strict on this policy and never offered counter-offers twice.

I saw Jill a couple of days after she had given her notice. She was flabbergasted. Every upper-level exec across all of the divisions of her company had called and written to her. She leaned on me to coach her through utilizing the energy that had been stirred up inside her once again, and she did it with success. Her current company gave her a surprising counter she couldn't refuse. More abundance, more freedom and more autonomy. It was something that had never been done at her company before but, despite the way they had treated her recently, they weren't willing to lose her.

The chances of what Jill pulled off happening were literally slim to none, if you look at what's "realistic." And yet, the chances of what Jill pulled off happening if you play by the rules of quantum vibes, was right on time. (Even, perhaps, divine timing.)

Also right on time is this message: the fact that *anything is possible*, even if it feels far-fetched and very unlikely.

Creating Big Energy Vibes

As human beings we can find it tough out there sometimes. But part of what makes life dynamic and interesting are the ups and downs of our feelings, experiences and situations. While we always want to aim for the highest vibes possible, it isn't, as I've said throughout this book, always going to be sunshine and roses. Jobs change. Relationships end. Loved ones pass away. Illness happens. Friends disappoint. All of these events, as well as plenty of others, can trigger us and shoot us down, down, down the Hertz Vibration Scale. The awesome part, though? We can repurpose the energy that arrives with these triggers in countless ways and on numerous levels.

Often, we try to push down all of our "low vibe" feelings. And, frankly, why wouldn't we want to? Rage, grief, distress, anxiety, bitterness are all uncomfortable to experience. When you turn up the volume on a radio or TV, the volume expands. It's like this with our energy too. The bigger you can allow your energy to get, the more powerful you become. With big energy we can vibe in the all-famous love zone *and* have space to process the more dense, lower vibe feelings. Where many of us go wrong here is we don't want to feel the uncomfortable feelings, so we numb or push them away, or get busy being busy and forget about them.

Shoving away these feelings isn't healthy; indeed, to paraphrase Carl Jung, what we resist not only persists but also grows in size. Avoiding our emotions is a form of numbing and it often, if not always, leads to other forms of numbing, whether that's going overboard on Moscow Mules, maxing out your credit limit at Saks, gambling your heart away online, exercising until you're in pain (and not the good kind), watching hours and hours of mindless television – you name it. We, collectively, need to choose healing and living, not numbing and deadening. That's what this whole programme is about.

We possess so many layers and aspects of ourselves and, as I've said in previous chapters, we can learn to view each of these parts of ourselves with acceptance, love and compassion. Once we do, we begin to alchemize the lower vibe feelings instead of pushing them deep down – which, let's face it, will one day explode in some sort of outburst. (Hello, hot-mess express I once was.)

No matter where we are on our journey, we're bound to be hit by triggers, just as Jill was in her career. It's simply part of the human experience. And, sometimes, adopting a positive outlook just won't cut it. If you want to grow, then you have to be willing to *process* triggers. So why not process them in a way that will catapult you toward your dreams and not down the rabbit hole of numbing out and victimhood?

Turning Your Triggers into Gold with Quantum Tool #5

In my fifth Quantum Tool, **Repurpose Your Energy**, we're going to take the stuff that triggers you and turn it into manifesting power. I don't know a single person who hasn't been triggered to some degree – throughout the pandemic, of course, but also in every other domain of life, such as career, love, finances, friendships, family, traffic, weather, the holidays, government, memories (and the list goes on and on).

Anger, fear, disgust, even sorrow can all be leveraged to achieve the very things our souls want. Triggers are some of our biggest impediments to bliss and accomplishment, whether it's fear of an unexpected lay-off, rage at the passive-aggressive comment our neighbour made, the anger that arises when our boss snaps at us, the annoyance we have for our spouse or room-mate after a never-ending quarantine together or misery when the lives we've planned are thwarted. And yet, triggers are also opportunities. They reveal the layers of energy inside us that still require healing and can fill us with inspiration and incentive.

If you don't know exactly what a trigger means, let me spell it out for you. A trigger is that feeling you get when your heart is beating fast, you feel so angry you could explode. The room and everything around you goes blank and something inside you comes boiling to the surface. You can't see straight, let alone think straight. Impulsivity sets in – and fiercely at that. In the heat of this moment you may break up with someone you genuinely love, end your lease because your landlord rubbed you up the wrong way, go into a road rage, grab that bottle of tequila after you've made it through Dry January, buy those shoes you really can't afford, text your toxic ex, quit your job on the spot or race through a red light. (In short, triggers frequently result in recklessness.) And the consequences of letting our triggers override us instead of work *for* us? Now that's something I *don't* need to spell out.

However, emotional triggers, are also sometimes called mental health or psychological triggers. These can be people, memories, even objects that almost instantly provoke strong negative emotions in us and are usually surprisingly intense.

Why does this happen? Because something in our past hasn't been properly processed and it erupts in the present when something sparks it off. Author of *Waking the Tiger*, Dr Peter Levine adds to this, even if he puts it slightly differently. He refers to triggers as "emotional memories" and says they're "echoes of memories stored in our bodies."

"The past lives in us in ways that we are often unaware of," he says. "Times when we may have been left alone, yelled at, hurt, neglected, abused, misunderstood, exposed to difficulty or otherwise traumatized, all leave imprints on our bodies that can last through many years and decades. The question is not whether these memories exist in us, but *how* they live in us."

To me a trigger is a part of you that needs some soothing. It's an element inside you that needs empathy, not shame or guilt or self-sabotage, and Levine would agree. Nor should a trigger serve as an excuse that may lead to an error, self-hatred or a straight-up catastrophe.

Rather, look at your trigger. Consider it an invitation to love yourself on a more profound level. Get curious about it, instead of mad at yourself for getting roused up. (Not *that* type of arousal!) Give the core emotion behind it a label, as naming your emotions can be extremely validating. Let your trigger show you what needs to be mended inside and then let it propel you closer to your dreams and desires.

You are human. You will absolutely have triggers. The question is, will you use them to spiral down the self-victim rabbit hole to more "low vibes" and numbing, or will you use them to bring awareness to your own evolution, to sit in the fire of what you are feeling and to ignite a passion within you that can only be instigated *by* your triggers?

When you look at Jill and how she chose the path of the empowered creator and the possibilities within the quantum field, of how she elected to repurpose her "low vibe," anger energy for the greater good of her happiness and freedom, you'll find that it's a beautiful example of what can happen in your own life when you're in your power and *you* get provoked.

Repurpose Your Energy – Today

I've coached, facilitated and led groups through transformational processes for more than 15,000-plus hours over the years. It is truly amazing to me what can happen when we bring intentional awareness to our energy and healing. Within this experience, what I have noticed most is that we give feelings a label they 100 per cent do not deserve. We label feelings as bad or good and that's not an accurate or productive method to follow. When we can start to view our feelings from a neutral perspective – from the place of an observer – we automatically turn up our vibrations. This is exactly what one of my best-loved exercises, Wheels in Your Heart, can do for you.

Let me explain this Wheels in Your Heart analogy – which, by the way, has been exceptionally helpful to me on my journey. The first thing you do is imagine your favourite car. Go big here! Think of a car that makes you smile, if not *grin*. There is no wrong or right here as long as it fills you with excitement and glee. Today mine is going to be a Porsche (I know if it was my nephews, they would choose a Bugatti or a Lambo!); there are other days when I desire a stretch limo. Choose what feels good to you at this moment.

Now, visualize the car in the centre of your chest, inside your heart. Go deeper. What does the car's interior look like? What colour is its paint? How fast can it go?

Then, picture the driver's seat of the car. Which part of you has the keys to the ignition? Your ego, your inner judge, your doubting self or your best self? Which part? Notice this without judgement and create space for each part of you in this car.

Back in 2013, when I was in my dark-night-of-the-soul moment, my fears and doubts definitely had the keys. The piece of me that cared so desperately what others thought of me, the one that was disappointed that I wasn't getting married after all, the one that felt empty – *that* version was in the driver's seat. Where was my heart? She was there, somewhere, most likely in the trunk buried under baskets and a yoga mat.

Today, though, my heart has the keys to the ignition. And I invite you to hand your heart the keys, too. As we notice these parts of us come to the surface, we don't need to shelve them, or "bad girl" (or "bad boy") them away. We just need to give them room to be seen and heard and loved. When we do this, we get to release the dark parts with love as well.

Jill is a great example of someone who was able to make space for her anger, to sit with the part of herself that felt betrayed by the company she had toiled away at for years. In honouring how she felt, instead of numbing the feeling, saying "I know," or just accepting the status quo, she gave her heart the keys to the ignition and created an opportunity for spaciousness, a quantum leap and a miracle.

This Wheels in Your Heart exercise allows you to see each part of yourself, each feeling, each piece of you – good, bad or ugly, if you will. It allows you to see yourself as whole, without giving unnecessary categorizations to the less appealing "ingredients." When we aren't shunning these pieces of us, they are given the liberty to be processed and set free. *Then* they can have a seat in the trunk, until it's time for the next layer of healing to begin and we get them back in a seat (with a seat belt on, mind you) until they have been heard and understood and loved. In other words, when we give the layers of ourselves a voice and recognition, we transmute and repurpose our energy, triggered or not, to align with our dreams and not with the old subconscious stories that aren't serving us.

Our psyche simply needs to be seen and listened to – even caressed. This is you. *You.* And you wouldn't be that vibrant, intricate, terrific, fascinating you if the areas of your psyche – the realms that create these triggers – didn't exist. Can you just imagine how flat we would all be if we didn't have "imperfections," hadn't made a single mistake in this sometimes-trying life or didn't have wants or needs, some of which may be "unconventional"? It would be like walking around in a world comprised of robots and Stepford Wives. In fact, I imagine that some of the coolest and most remarkable people you know are what naysayers might call "flawed." *You* know they're not. You know they're human, and prone to triggers and slip-ups. But I also imagine you're drawn to these people (think again of those compelling "high vibe" people I spoke of earlier) because they were vulnerable enough and strong enough to chill with their "low vibes." To deal with their triggers. To use what provoked them as a means to healing – and a reason, if not a crusade, to take them closer to freedom, meaning, pleasure and prosperity, however you might define it.

To recap, in Wheels in Your Heart, you visualize your big, beautiful, bold open heart in the driver's seat with the keys. This is the shiny side of you, the true and authentic piece of you; the one who is living in the top tiers of the scale where enlightenment and peace and joy and love prevail. Then, you notice the other parts of you have a place in the car too; they just don't get to have the keys. This is a powerful way to reprogram, rewire and repurpose your energy so that it is in alignment with your soul, passions and purpose.

All pieces of us are a portion of a greater consciousness. They're here in the name of the game we are playing in the school of Earth.

Why do I call it a school? Because that's what I believe it is. I also believe this is one of the largest, most glorious and also scariest voyages our souls can go on, being and learning and loving and vibing here. As a consciousness and a soul, we choose to come here for the purpose of learning to love more; to hit those top notes on the Hertz Vibration Scale and make a difference within our souls and the lives of others. When we think of life as a virtual reality, which it sort of is, we can see how we hold the controller and which buttons to push – and I don't mean this metaphorically. We have a choice; a lens that we create.

When you can shift your consciousness to understand this, you inevitably create a quantum moment. You elevate your energy to a higher perspective. You see things through an awakened state. You take that sadness and use it to create something tangible and lovely – say, a poem or a song – or call upon it when a friend has reached a similar place. (Hey you, empathy.) You take that resentment and exploit it to go after what you *really* want here on this planet – there's no point, after all, in being envious or mired in jealousy when anything is possible for you, too. And you take that amped-up anger and use it as energy to take yourself closer and closer to the person you want to be and all that person wants to achieve.

When your anger shows up, let it. Get mad, get annoyed. When the blues arrive, feel all the feelings. Do this with every "low vibe" energy that emerges. Grab your journal. Write 'em out of your body and onto paper. Name what you're feeling, even if you don't know the "why" behind it. (Again, think back to what I said about the capacity to heal with quantum leaps (see page 52.) Give your low vibes the front seat in your car but not the keys, then let these vibes drive you right back up the scale, even if it means you take a detour or a couple of steep hills along the way.

When things aren't working out for you, remember this: you have a choice. Always! Choose to write a new story and tell it. Then *live* it. Unlink and disconnect from the narrative that's not united with your desires and dreams.

Eradicate the shame and guilt that your triggers may have caused you in the past, because right here, right now, is the real start. Toss the pity parties out of the window and create from your internal reality where you hold the keys *and* the controller. Remember: *you* are in charge. *You* get to decide – not your boss, not your partner, not your family or best friend or what society tells you. You have the ability to bring awareness to any and all of the stories that aren't serving you. Because you, and you alone, have the power to turn your "low vibes" and triggers into downright gold.

QUANTUM TOOL #5
Repurpose Your Energy
RECAP

Let yourself feel your "low vibes" and utilize that energy to inspire a new solution you would never have thought of otherwise to find motivation, and to spur you into the quantum field. Give yourself permission to express yourself and claim your worth.

Your Blueprint for Positive Change

- The words "I know" will stall your manifesting game every time. Remain open to new ideas even if it means you need to experience some uncomfortable feelings and realizations.
- Fully feel your low vibes, then utilize the movement in that anger energy to inspire new solutions that can transport you into the quantum field.
- Triggers are big impediments to bliss and accomplishment, but they are also great opportunities for change. They have an upside – and an awesome one at that.
- When things aren't working out for you, remember you can *always* choose to write a new story, then create it and live it.

6

Activate Your Vision
in the NOW

*"The best way to predict your future is to create it
not from the known, but from the unknown. When
you get uncomfortable in the place of the unknown
– that's where the magic happens."*

Dr Joe Dispenza

QUANTUM TOOL #6

Stop playing the "I'll be happy when ..." game and get
yourself happy, even if it's only in your mind right now.
Soothe the heck out of your nervous system. Utilize
the power of your body and breathe energy into the
now moment. Feel your desires, activate the power of
visualization and become an energetic match to what
you covet.

Take a Quantum Leap

"Be. Here. Now." It's a statement many of us have come to know *exceptionally* well. Even if we don't practise the sentiment behind it, it often echoes in our heads thanks to the surge of memes, T-shirts, social media posts, bags and coffee mugs that feature it and fill us with inspiration. And while some might disregard the concept as a cliché, keep in mind that clichés become axioms for a reason: they have resonance, and often profound resonance at that.

Nothing could be truer than "be here now." It isn't an indictment, but a loving, encouraging insistence. As we've discussed, we often live either stuck in the past – with all of its heartbreak and regret and, for some (yours truly included), shame – or far-flung into the future, which, let's face it, rarely works out precisely as we schemed it. But being here now, totally present and wholly open to all of the realms of wonder and possibility, is in the end our only *real* option.

And yet, it's a gift we time and again do not relish. We have a fear of missing out (FOMO) instead of savouring what's right in front of us. Worse still, we're caught up in all those "agos," from "I shouldn't have said that" to "Why did I ever … ?" Or we future-trip into random scenarios – hello, catastrophic thinking – that likely will never happen.

The why behind our doing all of this is threefold.

1. Sometimes being alone can feel nerve-wracking because solitude forces us to confront things that would otherwise be shoved under the proverbial rug if we were surrounded by our family, colleagues and/or friends.
2. Psychologists suggest we ruminate about the past because we hope that, by thinking an experience through (even obsessing about it), we can change its result (and that's a *no way* if ever there was one).
3. Anxiety gives us a false sense of control over our future.

But the real question is: *Why* do we do this when all that we're looking for – peace, connection, joy and success – resides in the ever-present *now* moment?

Because, truly, the magic we desire is directly here before us, in the presence of and focusing on the now moment. As Thoreau once said, "You must live in the present, launch yourself on every wave, find your eternity in each moment. Fools stand on their island of opportunities and look toward another land. There is no other land; there is no other life but this."

At the same time – and this is where, I admit, it gets a bit tricky – to land where you want to go takes a quantum kind of vibe. It's in that now moment – exactly at this second – that you must be fully present, not just with your, well, presence, but also with who you want to become and what you want to achieve, whether it's a kick-ass promotion or a stronger sense of self-confidence and the rewards that come with it.

The Rearview Mirror is Not the Vibe

Years ago, I got super-acquainted with Dr Joe Dispenza's notion that in order to harness our ideal lives and selves, we must let go of the emotions and behaviours of the past and plug into the feelings and sensations of the future we desire.

This might sound strange, given that I'm also asking you to be as present as possible. And yet, simply cranking up your energy to the highest levels on that Hertz Vibration scale I bet you know by heart by now lets you do both. In fact, it *compels* it. It's quantum in nature, brilliant by design and an awesome rewiring exercise in both promise and imagination.

Here's how it works.

Picture yourself in your supreme spot. It doesn't have to be a place, per se, but hey, sometimes that works too, whether it's lounging in a hammock between two sun-dappled palms or at the summit of a snow-capped mountain. Wherever you are, you're happy. You're tranquil. You have financial freedom and a life cushioned by tons of love, support and inspiration. You're healthy in brain, body and conscience. You're empowered and at liberty. And, most of all, you're pumped to stay on this wonderful trajectory.

Now, how does the thought of this make you feel? (When I practise this, I usually feel warm and curious and blissful, even transfixed.) How does this space in time taste and smell? What kind of emotions are you feeling in this future version of yourself?

The point is this: your mind and the energy you both feel and emanate must arrive at this destination, however you might envision it, *before* you see it in your reality.

Can you breathe that in for a second? Really internalize it? Because, remember: you have the power to create your world with your own energy; with what you visualize, feel and concentrate on before it shows up in your 3D reality. It's the fifth dimension, and it's radically marvellous.

This is the magic of the quantum. You plug into where you want to go and hold onto the frequency it pledges, no matter what your circumstances.

And by "no matter what," I mean *no matter what* diversions might press themselves upon you, or how much angst you carry when you're not eyeing the top of the scale or what your current situation might be inciting within you.

Again, it's up to you; *completely* up to you. You are the controller of the game. When you play by others' rules and believe everything you hear on the news or are subjected to within our society (recall those naysayers we talked about?), you're not in charge. You're letting *them* dictate your energetic input and output.

But when you refuse to buy into others' judgements and limited beliefs, and begin engaging – really engaging –

with your brave, wild dreams? *Now* the dice is rolling in the appropriate direction.

The "I'll Be Happy When ..." Game

There are plenty of "games" we buy into. The games I mentioned above – the media and society, of course, which has only gotten more overwhelming since the advent of social media. There's also the game of allowing our subconscious minds to dominate and give in to our fears, even if they're so damaging they keep us from coming anywhere close to the finish line. The game of numbing and self-sabotage, too. And, of course, the game so many of us play: the "I'll be happy when ..." game.

You know this game, I'm sure; we all do. It goes something like this:

I'll be happy when ...

- I meet "my" ideal person.
- I'm bringing in X amount of money per month and my bank account is loaded.
- That new title at work is finally mine.
- I lose ten pounds (or, heck, *gain* for others).
- I move to a swankier spot.
- I can finally buy that Tesla Model S.
- I get back together with my ex.
- This pandemic is – oh my gawwwddd – at last *over*.

This game is addictive, to be sure, but it's also sly and bogus. It's an illusory carrot, with emphasis on *illusory*. Often, we place so much regret on the past and yearning on the future (and fixate on "getting there") that we lose sight of the journey, yes, but also of the beauty of the present.

What's worse, when you preoccupy yourself with the "I'll be happy when …" approach, you not only skip one of the keys to higher vibes – gratitude for this very minute – but you also create separateness.

When you're hankering for the desired thing from a state of "where *is* it?" you're subconsciously judging yourself for where you are in the moment. You may look at your peers and feel stung and resentful by all that they have – the house, the prestige, the partner, the kids, the clothes, the car, the ski boat – and feel like you're 100 miles south of satisfaction. This can evoke feelings of self-pity, as we all know, and when you play the victim role you feed into your judgements even more. In turn? You may regress to any or all of those games and prohibit yourself from any progress whatsoever.

I'm not gonna lie: I have to catch myself often on this one, when I am craving – if not begging – for something that is taking its sweet, sweet time to arrive.

And yet, you create cohesion when you transcend your judgement with love. You quantum leap your giant dreams into the now.

This is not to say that you should ignore the feelings that surface when you note you're not as far along on the path as you would like. Again, bringing these emotions to light is a central part of this programme. *Notice* that you feel separate. Let yourself feel it all! Invite the judgement into the wheels in your heart. Sit in the fire. Choose to let the discomfort of the blaze burn away the pieces that aren't in alignment with your heart and soul and authentic power. Understand it and alchemize it with love. Once you release the judgement, you create an internal overflow of love; and the more you follow this process, the higher the chances you'll feel so dang good you won't even need the material desire.

I heard a quote from my friend Phil Good on this topic and it really landed with me. He said, "The only reason you are still feeling stuck is because you are still judging yourself." I had an epiphany when he uttered these words. We have the power to activate LOVE in the now, simply by emancipating ourselves from internal verdicts and feeling our authentic power.

Your Golden Ticket

Not only is your authentic power the golden ticket to the quantum field, but it's also an energetic recipe for turbo-charging vibes that attract genuine manifestations.

How do you define it? Your authentic power is attuned to and connected with your heart. When you're struggling and searching – and it feels like nothing, absolutely nothing, is working out – it's usually because you're not connected to the power that resides in your heart. Why? Because it's been shrouded by veils of judgements and walls that were ostensibly erected to "protect" us – layers upon layers of stories that deceptively tell us we aren't good enough and we can't have the things we want. But when you feel content with what *is* and excited about where you're going? Now you're on the track to triumphs.

Our job is to uncover the false layers and inaccurate narratives and peel them back to reveal the raw, genuine truth. This feels scary, I know, because it's uncomfortable and unknown. It also feels scary because it means we're on the conduit to getting everything we've ever wanted – and success, for many, is synonymous with stress, even if it's precisely what we covet.

Why? Sometimes it's hard for our unconscious minds to vibe with just how good arriving at our dreams can be. But breathe it in. Allow it into your awareness. Let the delicious promise of it all sink in and galvanize your heart and energy, as you know by now, that you can create your ideal reality with your vibrations. It's a choice, literally every single day and every single moment *of* those days.

Let's dive into this deeper. Have you ever felt the full, unvarnished, authentic presence of another human being in front of you? They're listening intently, open and available to what you're saying. You feel seen and heard, buoyed and appreciated. I'd even say it's one of the most enchanting feelings and experiences we can experience.

Unfortunately, in today's world, these moments are hard to come by and fleeting for many. We're all so busy being busy, and that's a real shame because it's when we connect with others that we come alive and thrive. We rid ourselves of separateness. And it goes without saying that this disconnectedness has been severely compounded by the pandemic. Zoom Happy Hours, after all, rapidly lose their lustre.

In the work I do with my clients – both corporate and private, as well as the speeches I give on stage – what propels people toward breakthroughs is the presence and attention I show up with for them. It's as if once they have someone open their heart, see them and truly just be *present*, a whole new level of energy is unbolted. It expands their energy into a new and fresh way of being.

You could also call this "holding space" for someone. It's as if I or someone else who gives them this presence and attention pierces through all the personas they carry around and truly sees their heart, their soul. We hold a frequency that can energetically create a space leading to results for them through our presence in the now. It's the magic that our presence offers and the high-vibe energetics behind our intentions.

The person holding space for you could be someone who has already been where you want to go, holds the energy of what is truly possible and can help you see evidence of your dreams manifesting because they themselves have done it. It can be a team member you hired or work with who holds it all together when everything is falling apart.

They can help you have a mindset shift, which expands your capacity to receive and creates a new energetic "container." The best kind of containers are the ones in which it's safe to be who you really are; a vessel where you can feel both the good and the bad, periodically and at the same time; and a receptacle where it's safe to state your dreams and fears and even the silly little things that make you giggle. It's connection at its best.

True Connection Has the Power to Change the Modern World

This, I'm convinced, is what modern humanity is missing: connection with self, connection with each other, connection at work, connection within our communities, connection with nature and connection in all of our interpersonal relationships.

Fortunately, I'm often on the frontlines of connections at my programmes and retreats. The swiftness with which these bonds are formed blows my mind each and every time. Programme attendees and retreat-goers form connections that are far closer and more real than the relationships they have with those they most often share meals with. And most of the time? These ties occur within the space of a mere three days or even with someone they've only connected with via Zoom as part of a programme, and they often last for years, if not decades and beyond.

Connections of this magnitude happen because the people who show up for my programmes and retreats are ready for change, and inherently know that connection is part of a transformation's recipe. They're fiercely present, and whenever you put such solid energy into that "now" moment, you allow the quantum to be activated in your body. You become magnetic to a new type of vibration that just *is*.

"Wait a sec, Suzanne," you may be saying. "Quantum in your *body*?"

Hear me out.

When you're present and connected to the human in front of you, with your heart open, your judgement gone and your energy zeroed in on this person – *that* kind of present – you begin to transcend space and time. You create room in your physical self that organically calibrates to one of the highest frequencies of all: love. And the diffusion of love energy from your body into another soul works some extra magic. It electrifies the person with whom you're engaged, while also firing up your own wellbeing.

This is bringing your soul, your essence, who you truly are, into your experiences and allowing them to be felt by others. It's that love or above we discussed in the preceding chapters – that crazy, burning, beautiful high, high energy. It's the difference between greatness and legends and, *ah, le sigh*, just another concert, cheeseburger, movie, brunch with friends or goodnight kiss. It's capitalizing on *being here now*.

Right Here, Right Now

Let's get back to being here now. Have you ever watched a chef, your momma or dad or your partner flourishing in the kitchen as they prepare a meal? They've got rhythm, intensity, passion, and sheer, gorgeous presence. It doesn't matter if they're making a dish as gourmet as Confit of Moulard Duck or a simple cheese quesadilla: they're totally immersed in their tasks, flow and in *being*. You *feel* it in the food they make, let alone in seeing them wield a knife or cheese grater as they pull it all together.

Or have you ever attended a concert and you suddenly stop, so overcome with expansion and awe that you're rendered speechless, before your body starts moving, even if you don't like to dance, because the bass playing is *that* captivating? You close your eyes, and even with them shut, you feel that pure, primal energy? It's energy, alright – at the utmost frequency.

Or, have you ever gone to see a band and you laughed a little and maybe danced some but kept getting distracted by TikTok and your to-dos because the artist wasn't present and you were left feeling blasé about the whole event? Yep, that's energy too – only of the sort that you must avoid if you want to enter the flow and snap into quantum action.

I can definitely say that presence is something I have given naturally since I started going on stage and leading programmes for clients. I am my most present, focused and vulnerable when I'm speaking in front of a crowd or to clients. The transmissions that move through me honestly astonish me. It's exhilarating, it penetrates the hearts of those who are listening and it's felt by every person in the room or on the other side of the livestream, even if it's only experienced on a subconscious level. I love it when I see my audience's eyes widen. They lean in, and it grows so quiet in my pauses that you could hear a pin drop. Best part of all? I know that this absolute presence I'm bringing to the table is helping them as well. It's fortifying them with the knowledge of this book's very theme: *energy, heart and presence are everything*. They're the juice needed for flow in the moment, colossal shifts, and those huge, phenomenal quantum jumps into the spectacular.

Remember: we're human beings with energy that flows and moves through us, steadily, 24/7, like an electrical current. We're dynamic miracles capable of more than any of us realize. Our bodies are resilient. Our nervous systems were constructed to help us win, even if we experience emotional dysregulation when we're suspended on the lower bands of the Hertz Vibration Scale. Contemporary culture, on the other hand, attempts to cripple our strength, *if* we don't master the skills I'm sharing with you.

Many of these skills are rooted in our innate power to change our thoughts, behaviours, focus, energy, body and nervous system. We overlook this internal potency and fixate on distress and disappointment and fear instead. Even the 12-year-olds around us are feeling stress today. Pressure from social media, parents and peers – to be popular, to succeed in school, to do well in sports, to lure in the opposite sex and to look Instagram-worthy and stellar on that selfie through braces, breakouts and awkwardly-changing bodies – has grown to unprecedented pinnacles, with suicide risk, eating disorders, anxiety and depression at all-time highs. It's time to change this. First *you* learn and then you model it and share it with the generation below you.

When I look back at my own transformation, I see that I have been regulating my nervous system – and in an excellent way to boot – since 2013, nine years ago as I write this. I didn't quite know what I was doing at the beginning. But, as I discovered, the human body operates in a way where we can literally set ourselves up to expand energetically and feel happiness, fulfillment and peace simply through understanding the way it functions in the now moment.

Staying Focused on Your Desires in the Present with Quantum Tool #6

When we want something and it's not showing up, we get angry, stressed, teary-eyed, contrite, all the things my sixth Quantum Tool, **Activate Your Vision *in the NOW*** addresses, by reminding us of the power to be present, now. It teaches us to let in what I like to call "enough-ness" – starting this very second – to understand how to regulate our nervous systems now, and to let go of the illusion of certainty, also right now, while tapping into the glee and gratification our potential futures suggest.

This tool is all about amping up your inner game – the *good* game. It's about plunging even deeper into surrender and within your heart than you ever thought possible. In this place, you stop looking *outside* of yourself. You stop "waiting" to be stoked, meaning you leave that "I'll be happy when ..." game back in the past along with Monopoly and Beer Pong – and activate those high vibes found in the quantum field. You start jamming with the energies of "enough-ness" and terrific possibility. You stay focused on your desires, and you keep your energy plugged into those upper tiers on the scale as religiously as you would your iPhone charger. You own your truth and your authentic power, you open up the golden ticket of self-love and you swim in it like you never have before. You remember your true soul essence; you believe in infinite possibilities. You stimulate your energy and restore your nervous system with unwavering intention, in part by claiming "I am" statements:

- I am a powerful being who can create with my energy.
- I am made of love.
- I am a miracle and anything is possible.
- I am okay in this moment. Everything will be okay after this moment too.
- I am full of happiness and joy.
- I am living on purpose and I'm on a mission, attracting dreams I once believed were impossible.
- I am in the perfect place *right now*.
- I am on the most beautiful journey of self-discovery and everything is working out for me in this moment.
- I am keeping my eyes on the stars and my feet on the ground.
- I am creating a life that will blow my own mind, now, and in the scrumptious future.

These statements – and any others you come up with yourself – aren't platitudes. Empirical studies in neuroscience reveal that habitually repeating positive affirmations – like, really, truly practising them recurrently, if not daily – motivates self-integrity, self-efficacy (or, according to researchers, "our perceived ability to control moral outcomes and respond flexibly when our self-concept is threatened") and leads to enduring change. What's more, MRI evidence shows that particular neural pathways are increased when you engross yourself in the regular practice of saying positive affirmations. You can shift your vibe instantly! (A little science for you, if you want a fuller understanding of the concept: the ventromedial prefrontal cortex – the part of the brain associated with positive assessments and self-related info administration – becomes *more vigorous and lively* when we give thought and consideration to our strengths and values.)

What does all of this mean? It means that your mindset is absolutely critical to creating and manifesting your dreams, and that mindset is directly associated with the vibes you're exuding and feeling.

If you feel safe and calm, your energy can open even more and go even deeper into the quantum field, which enables you to become more and more of an energetic match to your desires. If you feel tense, disrupted, angry or reactive, you're in survival mode, and your nervous system is weighing whether you should fight, flight or freeze – which is not, it goes without saying, the state of mind and body to be in to pass through the golden gates of that radiant quantum field. It's about taking each and every tool you've learned here up to this point and going a level deeper, taking it into the now. The power of those "I am" statements will put you here, at this moment. Soothing your physical body and your nervous system will keep you there as well.

How? One way to reach that place of serenity where everything is possible is getting in touch with the polyvagal theory. Conceived by Dr Stephen Porges, a highly respected professor, researcher and scientist, the polyvagal theory proposes that activating your vagal nerve, the longest cranial nerve in your body and one that is directly associated with your nervous system, can rouse your parasympathetic nervous system (PNS) into action. The PNS represents the "rest and digest" functions in our bodies. This means we feel soothed, happy and connected. It means our nervous system isn't out of whack trying to regulate itself. This is key, as your PNS is the antithesis of your autonomic nervous system – the one that gets triggered when you're alarmed and provokes the need to either fight, flight or freeze.

When we can consciously understand how to create the feeling of comfort in our body, we shift into the now. How to use the polyvagal theory in your own life? A few exercises I like most are yogic breathing, jumping into a cold shower (which activates the vagus nerve), gargling (also an activation "button") and meditation. Emotional Freedom Technique (EFT) tapping – a method in which you "tap" nine crucial points on your body to alleviate anxiety and release traumatic memories – is also a great tool that can help with this. And once your PNS has been enlivened? You'll feel a sense of composure that'll ease you into higher energies.

Once "there" – or rather, in the rich, pleasurable *here* – give yourself permission to dream your biggest, most outrageous and seemingly implausible dreams. Unlock your mind so you stop playing those games and instead channel vastness.

Let's Play in the Field of Dreams

I'll be real: limitations was my middle name before my awakening. I was stalled in the mindset that it was futile to dream, even terrifying, because it rocks the boat, if you will; a perspective that exposes what no longer is (if it ever was) serving us. I was disconnected from what I sincerely wished for and covered it all up with multiple modes of numbing. If I did put the brakes on long enough to consider one of my dreams – and trust me, there are many on my mental desk – I didn't feel worthy of even *thinking* them, let alone seeing them manifest. I wouldn't speak these dreams out loud to my besties, nor would I allow myself to write them down. If anything, they felt like a distant speck in an empty field – certainly not a bright, quantum field kind of arena. It took every tool I'm providing you with in this book to see beyond the beyond. To stop listening to those cynics and critics. To return to the unbridled imagination of my childhood. To believe that these dreams were given to me because they were – and are – my real purpose.

That's the thing: if we have dreams in our heart, maybe to become a film director, a writer, a lawyer or a fabulous father or the leader of a non-profit, it's because God or the universe or however you might want to define *it* placed them in your heart. It is your reason for being; it is why you are alive. And to neglect that in the name of negativity – your own, as well as others' – is, well, doing an enormous disservice to humanity.

True, your logical mind – what I think of as our "cute, little mind," where playing small is misleadingly "mandatory" – will argue with this. It will tick off every reason it can latch onto to assert that your dreams are impossible, from "You don't have the time" to "You've hardly got enough talent/intelligence/skills/physical allure/ imagination for *that*." It'll say *you're never going to have that*. You don't *deserve* that home, job, partner, aptitude, Louboutin heels. Who do you think you are, really?

This logical mind isn't all that logical, ultimately. It's got a wicked negativity bias – an evolutionary prejudice that was fabricated to keep you out of harm's way – that obstructs you from realizing your dreams and keeps you away from the quantum field's brilliant rays. If you let your logical mind lead the way, you won't be connected to this moment or what your future promises or your heart, or, notably, the expansive vibes required to manifest your longings. Remember, there is no logic in the quantum field, only possibilities, and any and every possibility at that.

It's hardly news that the pandemic rocked us all. Whether we were barely eking out a living, crushing it professionally and privately or somewhere in the middle, we felt it. It was a time of transition and turmoil for everyone. Innumerable people – even, I'd say, the vast majority – were looking around at such bedlam and allowing their reality to create their energy. This is a disempowering tactic that slams you right down into the low-vibe pits where the quantum field seems questionable and days are defined by rage, agony and remorse instead of vitality, happiness and invention.

Invent Your New Reality

My process and this particular Quantum Tool specifically teach you to leverage your energy to invent your reality. Ignore what is happening around you if it sinks you. Learn to self-soothe and self-regulate your body and nervous system so that your biology can work in your utmost favour. And be ever-present and focused on the things that matter to you.

So many people were panicking during the pandemic and had no idea that these tools to help shift everything from their mindset to their emotional state even existed. My clients were blown away at the work we were doing together during this time. Several of my corporate clients were able to dial back to what really counted and rebuild a company culture that highlighted success and abundance. This was NOT the now the world was telling them they had to abide by, which was governed by fear and had little to do with their hearts' seeking.

Many of my other clients, those with both brick-and-mortar and online businesses, shifted their vision to a place that was much more aligned with their hearts, souls and passions. They rewrote the story of what was possible, gave themselves permission to dream and quantum leaped into a brighter, more certain future.

My own business changed in many ways, and I relied on this to offer inspiration to my clients. In 2019, I was on over 20 stages speaking to thousands – and this number doesn't include the more intimate workshops I led. As I've said, I love being on stage; it's where I feel my most lit up. At the same time, I realized I didn't want to move in that aggressive of a direction any longer – there's a lot of pull and pressure travelling the world to share your passions, purpose and process. There had to be, I told myself, a happy middle ground.

The quarantine and self-isolation that came with it made me, like everyone else on the planet, stir-crazy at first; never before had I really known how it felt to embody the term "cabin fever." And yet, by consistently returning to the now and not the worries of case numbers, death tolls, anticipatory grief and economic meltdowns, I had the capacity to see the silver lining of my circumstances. I was given the gift of stillness and a clean slate, as well as time to dive deeply into my heart and draw into consciousness some of my biggest dreams – dreams that I'd shelved because I didn't have the time or space to "indulge" them.

Activate Your Vision *in the NOW*

Years ago, I had written a novel loosely based on my revival, about a woman who went from an unaware, lost party girl to travelling the world on a mystical and magical soul retrieval mission led by the Divine, finding meaning, purpose and soul along the way. I dusted it off (or, rather, found it on my hard drive) and revised it with new-found clarity. That book, *Girl Awakened* (think: *Eat, Pray, Love* meets *Harry Potter*), was born.

I was finally given the space to launch this book and create a positive ripple effect in a brand new way. To this day, I feel immense happiness and gratitude every time I get a DM or a tag on Instagram from a *Girl Awakened* reader who is having their own mystical awakening. Indeed, there are few more gratifying feelings than touching the hearts and provoking the minds of others. And what better time to release a book about our inner game than in the darkness of a daunting, worldwide pandemic? Countless people told me that my novel gave them the hope and faith they needed to fire up their own transformations.

My point is this: *you* are the creator. You always have the choice of how you show up and what you give your energy to – and remember, your energy glows and increases magnetism the higher your energy goes.

My clients and I made a deliberate choice to stop looking at the toxicity of what the news was saying and the fear that was prevalent all around us. We started tuning into our hearts and pushing our energy levels up the scale. We tapped into big energy.

It's crucial to note that I'm not downplaying the fact that the world had been turned upside down. There's no arguing about that; we've all personally experienced or witnessed the deluge of heartache, misery, mental health conditions and loneliness the pandemic and its fallouts generated on the world stage. I'm not discounting that. I am simply saying that when we're faced with challenges, there's always an opportunity to change our attitude and energy in a more beneficial way – for ourselves, for those we love and also for the collective. "Be the change you want to see in the world," I'd tell myself and my clients during this era, following Gandhi's excellent advice. And we did – all by hoisting our vibes to greater heights.

I hope this is resonating with you, because if you can grasp this, you can manifest anything you want. It's that embodiment of turning up your vibration, of being in the energy and feeling it; and as you're feeling it, letting go of those narratives and games that aren't in alignment with what you want to achieve. Of shedding stale, constraining beliefs. Of attuning to the energy of what you desire and becoming that energy, that vibration in the here and now so that your dreams can manifest right before your eyes. This means being an energetic match to what you desire before it has materialized.

You might be thinking, *This sounds great and everything, Suzanne, but I am a planner, and I need to know how I am going to attract that increase in pay/feel more fulfilled/ persuade my kids to shift their behaviour/have my husband become more present/see that Benz show up in my driveway ...*

I understand this, it's common to wonder. But when you allow your vibration to go to *that* place of doubt where logical thinking dominates for too long, you close your heart and shut out the magnetism and power of your heart and the miracle of activating it in the now. When you get caught up in the *how*, you let your logical mind kick into high gear and take over your thoughts, emotions, vibrations and desires. Your nervous system springs into survival mode and you're granted momentum, sure, but it's in the wrong direction – and nowhere near the quantum field of infinite possibilities.

What I think 2020 did for me was teach me the powerful lesson that certainty is only an illusion. The truth is, we don't know if we will be breathing tomorrow, or even in another hour. There is no guarantee. We hope for health, love, success and abundance, but there will always be things that are out of our control that can snatch us off the path toward these ambitions. However, by becoming comfortable with the unknown, you also create space for the universe to surprise you. Your job is to be so bonded to your vision that you don't even need to know the means of how you'll get there. You just trust that you will. That's what dreams are, really; and we realize them by steadfastly believing in them and feeling them on a bone-deep level. That is part of becoming an energetic match. Your energy matches your desires before you have actualized the desire.

And that permission to dream, despite it all? It'll move your energy into the now, where you can "try on" your future, feel all its good feelings and use your positivity as the world's most auspicious engine. I'll say it again: connect with your heart and let it lead you.

So, here's my advice, if not my loving command: *be here now*. Be so present you don't even know what day it is. Saturate your physical, mental, psychological and energetic self with affection and admiration. Halt that "I'll be happy when …" game and accept that happiness is here, now, for your taking. Love all of you exactly as you are, even if you feel "behind" or "unworthy." (Slay those thoughts, *puh-lease*.) Stop peering into those rabbit holes to see what's "realistic" and instead refocus on the present's joy and the future's possibilities.

Start pulling up those dreams from the depths they've been buried in. Let them *fill* you. Permit them to prompt you to think – and, more importantly, *feel* – what your future has in store for you. Operate in the now, as if your future and all that you wish to accomplish has happened. By promoting the necessary mindset to achieve what you want – by choosing to believe that your desired outcome has already occurred – your observations and sensory experiences and emotions will begin to manifest the life you've long been after. How, in this place, would your days unfold? What does that smile look like on your face? How do you feel from head-to-toe, and in your soul? High-vibed, I'd propose, because somewhere, in the now, you know that if you follow the tools I am teaching you, your dreams will show up. And if they take their sweet, sweet time to arrive? Keep quantum leaping forward, and trust in the timing of the Divine.

QUANTUM TOOL #6
Activate Your Vision *in the NOW*
RECAP

Stop playing the "I'll be happy when ..." game and *get* yourself happy, even if it's only in your mind right now. Soothe the heck out of your nervous system. Utilize the power of your body and breathe energy into the now moment. Feel your desires, activate the power of visualization and become an energetic match to what you covet.

Your Blueprint for Positive Change

- Happiness, peace, connection, joy and success reside in the ever-present *NOW* moment. Infusing your presence in each task and hobby you are doing collapses time and expands energy, creating an exciting experience.
- When you're present and connected to a fellow human being, with your heart open and your energy focused on them alone, you calibrate to one of the highest frequencies of all – love.
- Expand your authentic power by connecting with your heart and soul now and aligning your personality with your soul in each *now* moment.

- Opening your heart and creating true heartfelt connections in your life will not only create more meaning and purpose but will truly assist in helping the modern world to be a happier and more peaceful place.

7

Follow the Flow of Synchronicity and Divine Guidance

"If you knew who walks beside you on this path that you have chosen, fear would be impossible."

Helen Schucman, *A Course in Miracles*

QUANTUM TOOL #7

There is so much in this world we live in that we can't experience through our senses. Open your heart and look for the signs, synchronicities and "coincidences" to find your flow and get in the jet stream of miracles and magic.

She Talks to Angels

In February 2019, I had another moment – you know, those moments that fire up something of a personal revolution. I stepped outside in a charming little town on the coast of California, after finishing an event I had spoken at in a town nearby the weekend before. The air felt fresh, the sun ultra-soothing. My heart began to flutter. I peered across the street at one of the most gorgeous coastline views I had ever seen. The ocean was sapphire blue; the sun danced on the water like diamonds. The cool ocean breeze moved across my skin. Oh, the *possibilities* my mind fixed onto, as the wind blew through my hair. A deep inner knowing overcame me as I stood there, transfixed. I could feel my intuition telling me that *this* was precisely where I was supposed to be.

Alright, intuition, I'm down, I thought. *Totally down. This place is amazing.*

Such thoughts filled me as I walked to a coffee shop, the cute-as-can-be café rich with the aroma of fresh brews and ground beans. People milled happily about, while just outside those vistas continued to glitter. I was smitten; positively enamoured.

I spent the next two weeks in this enchanting, quirky beach town. I fell in love with it more and more each and every day. While I was based in Atlanta, Georgia, I had spent the last decade travelling the world. And while my heart craved more travel and adventure as soon as my trips ended, I was always ready to return home, to a place that epitomized "sanctuary." (Yes, those massive remodels finally came to fruition!)

This trip was different, though. I had been away from Atlanta for two and a half weeks and when Sunday rolled around and it was time for me to head to the airport, I dreaded leaving. I pulled out my calendar to see if I could arrange to stay longer. It wasn't an option. I had a full week of clients and appointments, and a stage to speak on in Atlanta the following week.

Begrudgingly, I hopped into a cab and went to the airport. This was a strange feeling for me; it was entirely new. I had never felt like this on my way home before.

When I pulled into my driveway at midnight, I still couldn't shake the feeling – I was usually thrilled to get back to my creature comforts and the objects and furniture I had so carefully selected, purchased and nurtured. Something inside me urged me to get out my computer and research available properties in that charming little town, instead of curling up on the sofa with a book like I tend to do when I need to decompress after a trip. I typed in the zip code of that quaint, lovely beach town I was already missing desperately and browsed property after property, growing more besotted with the place with each listing.

It was instinctual, this – and I was listening. My heart knew where my soul was taking me. It was almost as if I didn't have a choice in the matter.

Monday started with a bang and didn't stop. The week was fast and furious. I ended up baring my soul on stage at my event, where I shared my new-found desire to pack up and head west, that California ache *in my heart* to quote Led Zeppelin.

I also fessed up to all of the fears that this newborn longing was stirring up in me. My soul would say, "Go, girl, go! This is what you've been dreaming of!" Then my logical mind would chime in and start nattering away like a hyper-talkative passenger sitting next to me on a plane. *What do you think you're doing? Everything you know is in Georgia! You built and created your oasis. Your family is here, your friends, your community, your support system – your world.*

My heart and soul, timid at first, would pipe back in: *Remember all those vision boards you did? They're teeming with ocean views! Remember how at home you felt on that shore and walking along those beautiful beaches and streets?*

It was a struggle, this internal wrestling match, and it threw me down into the lower tiers on the Hertz Vibration Scale. I knew what my heart and soul wanted but my logical mind refused to oblige. I didn't know the "how" behind setting up shop 2,188 miles away from all that I had long cherished. To take that plunge into the unknown? It would be exhilarating, to be sure, but it was also downright terrifying.

I rearranged my schedule and spent some time working from the West Coast that April to "try on" the place. (A dress rehearsal in one of the sweetest spots I'd ever visited? It wasn't hard to persuade myself.) Once there, my soul felt electrified. The town, the beach, the people, the environs – all of it freed and energized me. Plus, going on a lone adventure and exploring a new area? Talk about a way to have fun and to hone my vision.

And yet, I still wasn't clear on what I should do when I returned home to Atlanta. Why was my heart so sure, but the rest of me still so doubtful? I needed a sign, something that would tell me if I should take one of the biggest chances of my life or bloom where I had roots.

Why? Because I firmly believe that we're always being guided and led, *if* we open our eyes and are willing to let in this direction. I believe there's a higher power that possesses a bird's eye view – a broader, entirely different perspective – and is piloting our course from afar.

A Little (Well, Actually, Large) Bird Told Me So

Shortly after I got back into the swing of things at home, I started prepping for the following day's speaking event. It was 5:55am – too early for even a speck of sunlight – and I jumped up in bed. From somewhere unidentifiable came a loud *bam, bam, bam.* My head spun as I searched around. What *was* that? There wasn't any construction going on near my home; besides, who in their right mind would be hammering away before 6am?

The *bam bam bam* continued and so did my annoyance. My mornings are sacred: precious time in which I set intentions, align my energy and meditate. The *bams* didn't fit in so well with my routine. In fact, they rather shattered it.

I eventually tuned out the noise, used my earbuds to meditate and went about my day. The next morning was the first day of the event and I needed to be on my A-game. Guess what? 5:55am and that *bam bam bam* shook me out of my much-needed sleep again. What the heck *is* that? I asked the ceiling. And why is it so loud?

The ceiling, by the way, didn't answer.

I breathed. I tried to do a light bath meditation only to be jolted by another *bam bam bam*. It felt like my house was literally shaking. The glam squad had just pulled up to get me ready for the stage and I needed to meditate and read my notes one last time. Whatever that noise was, it wasn't going to get in my way today, I told myself.

And it didn't. I had an excellent time with the attendees of the event and shared that I was awaiting a sign to guide me for what might be the next chapter of my life.

Day Two of the event and this time I wasn't even surprised by the earsplitting, totally unpleasant wake-up call, again exactly at 5:55am. *Bam bam bam.*

Instead of bemoaning the racket, I got up, determined. I *had* to figure out the source of this clamour. I followed the sound and walked onto my deck … only to find a large woodpecker going to town on the super-expensive cedar beams that made my deck elegant. I went outside and shooed it away, exasperated by this pesky, persistent bird.

Once again, the show must go on, I reminded myself. I had people to serve and inspire. I used my tools – the very ones you've been digesting throughout the course of this book – to shift my energy back into a positive space. It worked: the event was nothing less than potent and transformational.

The morning after the event, my resident woodpecker decided to let me sleep in a whole extra 49 minutes and didn't bother showing up until 6:44am. Either that, or he was quiet for the first part of his visit. Then it was *bam bam bam* and more *bam bam bams*. Now I was straight-up annoyed. I tried to shoo him away again, but he wasn't scared of me. In fact, Mr Woodpecker – I was convinced it was a he – had only grown bolder overnight. He looked me dead in the eye and spat out a chunk of my exquisite cedar beams *right at my feet*.

I froze. Not because I was scared of this bird (I had grown up in the woods, as you might remember), but because an inner voice suddenly *bammed* away inside me too, even louder and more insistent than this creature by my toes.

Google the meaning of woodpecker, it said.

I rushed inside and went straight to my laptop. The spiritual significance of my very annoying alarm clock hit me like a ton of bricks:

"The symbolism of a woodpecker suggests it's time to pay attention because an opportunity has come knocking. In other words, the woodpecker is signalling you that great changes are afoot in your life. Therefore, you must seize the moment. The door is wide open for you right now and success is yours for the taking."

Oh my goodness, I thought. *Are you serious?* This was the sign I had been asking for – and it was crystal-freaking-clear. I felt annoyed and angry at myself that an animal literally had to start tearing apart my home to get my attention. There wasn't a subtle thing about it.

And then I felt thrilled. This, all of this, had happened for a reason.

Signs, Signs Everywhere

Regardless of what you believe, I guarantee you've been led or guided by a sign in your life as well. Signs, synchronicities, repetitions all exist to show and reassure us we're either on the right path or may need to head in the other direction. They're prevalent in numerous cultures, from Hawaiians' belief in *aumakua* (family gods, often ancestors, who arrive in the form of an animal and are considered omens that save people from harm) to Native Americans' profound belief in interpreting dreams and going on solo vision quests, during which their environment provides clues about a person's direction and character.

Carl Jung himself was a big believer in these messages from the universe and defined synchronicities as "meaningful coincidences of two or more events where something other than the probability of chance is involved." He thought that these signs reflect psychological processes, offer messages in the same sense that dreams often do, and take on meaning and give guidance that parallel our emotional state, or what I like to think of as our heart and soul.

Translation? More intuition. Less intellect. And in that moment, my hand covering my mouth as I went down the rabbit hole of the implications of the woodpecker, I had luminous clarity on what my next steps should and would be. And after that realization, I never heard the *bam bam bams* again. The message had been received.

Over the next few months, I travelled widely, speaking both in person and virtually, exploring one of the most splendid European vistas and spas I'd ever seen. (Remember that special moment in the Italian mountains?) Once I returned home, I booked a one-way ticket to California, packed a few suitcases, got my home ready to rent and followed my heart into the great unknown. I didn't know a soul in the beach town that had enraptured me, save for a few baristas and bartenders I'd chatted with at the cafés and restaurants I had ventured to on my visits. But I did know I felt more alive and on fire than I had in recent memory; that I was more than ready to see what would unfold for me. It was rare for me to do something quite so audacious with so little certainty. But when I had made these "power moves" in the past, they had ultimately ended up being pivotal, powerful turning points in my life. I didn't know where I was going to live in this sun-splashed new place, or how it would all shake out; but I knew, on a cellular level and with my entire being, that *this* is where the universe was leading me. It called too much to my heart to ignore it.

I began looking for places to live. In hindsight, I didn't let myself dream big enough. I wanted some sort of ocean view. A peek-a-boo glimpse from my kitchen window was good enough for me. I also wanted to be able to walk to the ocean, to feel the warm sand on my skin as often as possible. I loved the idea of being able to walk downtown and have access to shops and restaurants too.

I felt alive and free and excited about new possibilities. I plugged my energy into the feeling I wanted to sustain and let myself be guided each step of the way.

After about two weeks into my search, I came across an agent who gleefully shared over the phone, "I have the perfect place for you, based on everything you've told me."

It was indeed perfect. It was also three times above the budget I had set for myself.

Still, I went to see it. I found myself admiring the palm trees and serene ocean waves on my way to meet her. As I walked through the gate of the place she had found for me, I felt the cool ocean breeze blowing through my hair – the same sensation I had had when I visited in February. My heart fluttered again, but at a faster pace. An open path led straight to the ocean. *Oh my goodness, yes, please!* I walked inside and my jaw dropped at the floor-to-ceiling windows across the entire place. All that was on the other side was the vast, gorgeous, open, brilliant-blue ocean. My heart skipped another beat. I breathed a sigh of disbelief as I realized I was standing in the very middle of my vision board.

Of course, I wanted the place on the spot, but it was much more than I had anticipated spending. All logic told me to pass and get something more "realistic." Every bone in my body, meanwhile, said, THIS is what life is about. This is a quantum leap right into one of your biggest, wildest dreams. I understood the power of leaning into guidance and uncertainty and decided that maybe, just maybe, it was time to let more love in and live my dream. To follow my desire to begin a new life that would catapult me, again and again, into quantum moments of bliss. I turned to the agent with a grin and said, "I'll take it."

Tuning into Messages from the Universe with Quantum Tool #7

My seventh Quantum Tool may be the most under-estimated of all. I am asking you to **Follow the Flow of Synchronicity and Divine Guidance**. It's a tool to remind yourself often that it's not just "smart" but imperative to pay attention to the signs, symbols and synchronicities that abound around us if we're mindful and "tuned in," not only to the right energetic frequency but also to the universe. I could have continued getting irate at that galling, adamant woodpecker and still be living in Atlanta with half of my mind obsessed with this town in the West. Instead, by opening up to the lure of the quantum field – and listening to both my heart and the universe's guidance – I saw that woodpecker as magic. Sheer magic. He prompted monumental change and slung me into the flow of manifesting my bold, big, exciting dreams.

Think of it this way: swimming against the tide, walking against the wind and interrupting the momentum of positive occurrences through self-destructive behaviours are all forms of resistance that deplete our energy faster than a wave can tear us off our surfboard (and you needn't be a surfer to realize this).

But if we position our boards correctly, surrender and trust in our strength, intuition and true, heartfelt desires, we can ride joyfully to shore and nail the happiness and sense of accomplishment our hearts desire.

Another way to look at it is this: we live in a world ruled by movement – think of how everything, even inanimate objects, are roiling with energy – and if we fight against it instead of going with the natural, divine flow of it, we're bound to experience the same frustration that put us so far away from our dreams in the first place.

"Flow" can be as simple as five green lights in a row, a parking spot opening up in the front row of a stadium on game day, having a friend text right after you think of them or seeing the same numbers or objects over and over again.

It can also be as complicated as an animal nearly tearing down your house to snag your attention.

The gist is that when we vibe with the natural rhythm of the universe, life starts to get really fun; what some psychologists call "cosmic cairns." They're winks and nods from the universe, which is assuring you that it is, indeed, holding your hand. That it does in fact have your back.

In this Quantum Tool, I want to take it a step further and delve into the invisible force I believe is guiding us. This tool has been a huge game changer for me in all areas of my life. It's as if I have a special mentor who lives inside my heart and all around me. A mentor, a friend even, who can see things I can't; who can understand things my logical brain (that cute, little mind) could never comprehend as guidance; as comfort that I've chosen the correct fork in the road.

This guidance comes in various shapes, sizes and forms. When writing my novel, *Girl Awakened*, I received such strong, intuitive, spiritual downloads that I was often left breathless. They ran through me at lightning speed – so much so it seemed the book was writing itself.

One writing day, however, I felt stuck, even a little blocked. The blank page stared back at me, begging something of me I didn't have. My brain felt dulled; my attempts at writing sentences, weak. Where did the inspiration, the fire, go? I was puzzled because this was the first time it had happened and the book was nearly finished.

I mentioned my struggle to my sister Valerie. And she replied, "Suz, have you tried listening to classical music while you write?"

Her words resonated with me on a visceral level, but they were also incongruous with her character. Val prefers Bryan (as in Luke) to Bach and Michael (as in Jackson) to Mozart. Indeed, I had never in my life heard her listening to classical music.

Still, I gave it a shot, and guess what? It worked! The flow and effortless rhythm returned immediately. My fingers glided across my keyboard as if they were dancing.

A few days later, Val overheard me telling someone about this episode and her sage advice. "I didn't say that," she said, butting into our conversation.

I turned to look at her. "Yes, you did."

"No, I don't think I did ..."

"Val, you did! Why would I make this up? I was standing over by the window in the kitchen stirring a pot of spaghetti I had just made. I remember it clear as day."

She frowned at me and shook her head and it struck me: my sister had been used as my sign, as a vessel or a messenger. Something divine had seen an opportunity to flow through her to help me. And she didn't even remember – why would she? It was a message for me, and it had been received.

Another colossal sign landed for me a short time ago. I was feeling a little sad about the dissolution of my relationship with Matt. Truth was, I missed him. We had a ton of fun together and I longed for those times again. Since parting ways, he'd reached out here and there, and in our most recent exchange, he asked if we could get back together. My heart skipped a beat and I instantly felt butterflies in my tummy, only I didn't know what they were telling me. Even though I knew he wasn't my Mr Right, I also knew it would be awesome to see him again.

And yet, after I had said yes and he had reached out to make plans, his tone seemed nonchalant at best. It didn't light me up; it didn't make me feel great. This was partly due to his timing: he had texted me at the last minute to get together. I already had a date that evening and so I had asked him if we could try for the next day. We agreed to connect the following afternoon.

I didn't agonize about it necessarily, but I also didn't feel terribly excited. When I saw him, something went flat inside me. It was the first time I had seen him where there was zero attraction pulsing through my body; as if the chemical bond between us had been irrevocably busted. It was odd and unnerving. A palpable disconnect and distance echoed between us. It was as if I was still cheering him on, I still wanted the best for him, but the feelings – the connection and allure – had vanished. Maybe it was because he wasn't in fierce pursuit of me the way he had once been, or perhaps the timing just wasn't right for us. I accepted these things, but I couldn't help the disappointment and grief that arrived with this realization. Still, I thought, maybe there was a chance for us. Perhaps we could turn a corner and reignite what we'd had.

After our disheartening date, I found some random trash – red paper and I don't know what else – in front of my door, likely from one of my neighbours having a party.

Annoyed, I rolled my eyes and walked right past it. The next morning on my way to savour one of my favourite Saturday morning rituals of going to the farmers' market, I noticed the same red paper sitting on the pathway to my doorstep. Normally I would have picked it up and thrown it away. I didn't. I walked right over it and went on to enjoy perusing veggies and fresh fruits before meeting a friend for brunch. It wasn't like my neighbours to drop trash at my door, but such is life, right?

On my way back home, I stepped over the red paper again. This time I stopped in my tracks when I looked down and saw the most beautiful, heart-shaped green crystal on my doorstep. It was small, about the size of a quarter, but nonetheless noteworthy – another sign, I was sure of it. I mean, a green heart-shaped crystal on my doorstep? It had to be a good omen.

Then my heart sank. I turned around and noticed the red paper and trash I had been stepping over were triangles. Literally red shaped triangles. Are you kidding me? Two red flags! Like, actual *flags*.

Clarity descended. The red flags represented what I was feeling when it came to my relationship with Matt. I already knew he wasn't my person. With his indifference, he was showing me the same too.

The red flags and the way I felt when I saw Matt were all I needed to finally close the door on our relationship. Don't get me wrong. I will always wish Matt success and happiness. He will hold a special place in my heart forever. But the Divine wanted me to know my green heart was in front of me and not behind. My future was beckoning, and my past – well, it was just that: the past.

Galvanized, I stepped through my door, gazed at the ocean view that always served as my succour and strength, and settled into that glorious, delicious feeling of knowing I was making precisely the right decision, much like I did when I decided to uproot my life in Atlanta or flip my career upside down and answer my soul's calling.

Follow the Flow of Synchronicity and Divine Guidance

You can tune in to the same synchronicity and divine guidance as I did in the situations I've described above.

What if you decided that today is the beginning of your new chapter in life? What if you decided, starting TODAY, that the next ten years are going to be the best ten years of your life? In this declaration you invite in a new high vibe – an unseen power that has unlimited access to the quantum field, its ever-knowing energy influencing you and steering you into the realm of love and above and wonderful possibilities. What if you took all the tools I've given you, utilized them and embodied them? You would welcome an invisible superhero type of power into your life to guide you toward your dreams – *that's* what you would be doing.

Ask yourself what might seem possible in this moment that seemed impossible only yesterday. What if it all works out? What would your life ultimately look like? Beautiful, I imagine, and so very you.

QUANTUM TOOL #7
Follow the Flow of Synchronicity and Divine Guidance
RECAP

There is so much to this world we live in that we can't experience through our senses. Open your heart and look for the signs, synchronicities and "coincidences" to find your flow and get in the jet stream of miracles and magic.

Your Blueprint for Positive Change

- You are being guided by an all-knowing, powerful, invisible force that absolutely has your back.
- Signs, synchronicities and repetitions all exist to show and reassure us we're either on the right path or need to head in another direction.
- Think of how everything, even inanimate objects, vibrate with energy – and go with the natural, divine flow of it. You have the power to do the same.
- Declare your intention to change your life today and invite in that unseen power with unlimited access to the quantum field and the jet stream of miracles and magic to be your guide.

Quantum Tool Recap

Before you move on to the exercises in the Workbook section, here's a quick reminder of all those powerful, life-changing Quantum Tools you will be putting into practice.

Quantum Tool #1:
Turn Up Your Vibrational Frequency

This involves looking at where you are in life and taking it to the next level. You turn up the vibration of the energy you're emitting by feeling your emotions and focusing on the good that is directly in front of you. You understand that you have the power in any moment at any time to shift your vibration and expand your energy.

Quantum Tool #2:
Connect to the Quantum Field

Here you focus your energy on your dreams, align your personality with your heart and soul and pay more attention to infinite possibilities instead of all the reasons in front of you that make you think things aren't working – even if those limits are entirely within yourself. You dance and play in the field of dreams and connect to the desires of your heart. You understand that there is an infinite quantum field of possibilities ready and available for you to connect with and draw toward you. You've got this.

Quantum Tool #3:
Align with Love or Above

With this tool you practise feeling more happiness and worthiness and allowing the good feelings in. You commit to treating yourself the way you would treat the person you love most with kind words, empathetic actions or simply a treat that will nourish your body, mind and spirit. When you fall away from love energy, you rebound as quickly as possible by comforting your feelings with presence and compassion. You allow yourself to let more love flow into your life in all areas, so you can then give an outpouring of love to the people you love and serve.

Quantum Tool #4:
Reprogram and Rewire Your Mind

Here, you create a superpower by understanding the way your mind works. When things are not happening for you, you go within and look at the mental loop or programmed stories that are not in alignment with your big, beautiful dreams. You take your power back and begin to tell a new story by creating a fresh narrative that will take you where you want to go and you make sure that it's far, imaginative and everything you've ever dreamed of. It's where you're meant to be. You understand how to access the subconscious mind and you use it to help you manifest your desires.

Quantum Tool #5:
Repurpose Your Energy

This involves letting yourself feel your "low vibes" and allowing that energy to activate and inspire a new solution you would never have thought of otherwise to find motivation and spur you into the quantum field. You give yourself permission to express yourself and claim your worth. You also discover that triggers have an awesome upside when you harness this Quantum Tool!

Quantum Tool #6:
Activate Your Vision *in the NOW*

This is where you stop playing the "I'll be happy when …" game and *get* yourself happy *now*, even if it's only in your mind at present. You also: soothe the heck out of your nervous system; utilize the power of your body and breathe energy into the now moment; and feel your desires by activating the power of visualization and becoming an energetic match to what you covet.

Quantum Tool #7:
Follow the Flow of Synchronicity and Divine Guidance

And finally, you open your heart and look for the signs, synchronicities and "coincidences" to find your flow and get in the jet stream of miracles and magic. You trust and know that there is a higher plan at play and that you are always being guided.

PART TWO

THE QUANTUM VIBES WORKBOOK

Introduction to the Workbook

Welcome to the next sensational stage of your life! You have officially journeyed with me through each of the seven Quantum Tools, as well as my own and some of my clients' experiences of using them to turn up our energy and vibrations in a powerful way.

This next section and guidebook is a blueprint for creating positive change and is designed to help you up-level your existence, harness your inner power and create a life that blows your mind *all of the time*. By performing the following practices and exercises on a conscious, consistent basis, you'll dial up your internal frequency, feel electrified and become an energetic match to everything your heart desires.

The thing about the Quantum Tools is that they never expire. As long as we are breathing, we are growing. I have used these tools for years now and I still use them to this day. Here's the secret sauce to these tools: victory – and the realization of your boldest, biggest dreams – happens in the *commitment* and in actually using and implementing what you have learned. Remember that energy flows where your *attention* goes.

Scientific findings back this. Data demonstrates that repeating a new pattern for 30 days creates new neural pathways in your brain – a super-excellent thing, as they promote the creation of fresh, positive habits. These new neural pathways will allow you to unite your conscious and subconscious minds and compel them to work together in concert. This will naturally translate to embodying the energy of *precisely* what you want to call into your life.

My recommendation is that you dive deep into one Quantum Tool per week for the first six Quantum Tools. Focusing on one per week will give you time to get to know and be able to repeat the meditations and exercises – and to build a solid foundation as you work your way up from the first Quantum Tool to the sixth. But this is only a guide; if you feel you need to take longer on each or any Quantum Tool, go ahead. The seventh Quantum Tool is to assist you in staying on track and in the jet stream of miracles. (Think of it as maintenance.)

I suggest that you work through the whole sequence of practices and exercises in this Workbook at least once. Once you have done that, you can return to it whenever you want or if you feel you need assistance with one particular tool. Similarly, you may find that one tool resonates more with you than others. If so, amplify your power by returning to it time and again and as much as you like.

But these tools aren't just here for you in the moment or only when you're vibing down. They are here to take you to your next level, and then the next after that. As long as you want to keep taking quantum leaps into places that will blow your mind, these tools will be here to help you. Use them and tap into them anytime, anywhere – whether you need to refresh your energy, rediscover your motivation or encounter a situation that leaves you craving for more solid footing on the ground.

With some of the exercises in the following pages, I'll recommend an essential oil to boost your vibe even further. According to researchers using the Tainio Technology frequency monitor, which was developed by a biologist, chemist and expert on sustainable agriculture at the Eastern Washington University Cheney, USA, the vibrational frequency of essential oils is the highest of any natural known substance. Essential oils are an easy and proven way to release stuck emotions, heal old thought patterns, clean out your energy field and instantly call a high-calibre vibration into your space. (If you don't have the essential oils recommended here, you can always fold them into your personal programme later. This is an optional suggestion to enhance the tools, but it isn't necessary to have them in order to see real, oh wow! results.)

Grab a journal and a pen or open the notes section on your phone or iPad, expand your heart and begin to expect miracles, magic and massive breakthroughs. This is your arsenal for a happier, more gratifying and exhilarating life. Get ready to dig in, turn up your vibes and feel inspired!

Week 1

Quantum Tool #1:
Turn Up Your Vibrational Frequency

This Quantum Tool is all about turning up your vibration so that you're hovering near the top – if not at the acme – of the Hertz Vibration Scale – see page xxv). (Remember, you can take another look at the scale at any point to refresh your memory and see where you think you land. And you can refer to it as often as you like.)

In order to elevate your vibration, you first need to know what dominant energy/vibration you're carrying right now.

How?

By taking an inventory of how you feel and where you "spend" the majority of your time in these vibration fields, which you can see once again in the diagram of the Hertz Vibration Scale overleaf.

Now, in this moment, glance at the scale and gauge where you fall on it. Notice without judgement and be kind to yourself. Now think of a time this week when you might have behaved in a way that you aren't very proud of. Where did you land on the scale in that moment? What about a time in the last week when you felt very happy?

THE HAWKINS HERTZ SCALE

Hz	
700+	Enlightenment
600	Peace
540	Joy
500	Love
400	Reason
350	Acceptance
310	Willingness
250	Neutrality
200	Courage
175	Pride
150	Anger
125	Desire
100	Fear
75	Grief
50	Apathy
30	Guilt
20	Shame

Higher Frequency

Lower Frequency

Maybe when someone you love did something to pamper you, or you got to enjoy a special moment in nature or a romantic kiss with your special someone. Where were you on the scale in that moment? Keep in mind that your vibrations change day by day and often several *times* a day. Still, being truthful here and noting where you usually are works as a terrific barometer of your emotional range and energetic state.

Perhaps you feel apathetic about work because you've hit a plateau and are awaiting a fresh project that'll reinvigorate you. Maybe you are feeling the Joy vibes because you've recently met or exceeded a health goal and toned your biceps or have hit your target savings amount. Quite possibly, you are feeling aligned with Courage because, well, you're holding this book in your hands – and any sort of personal enhancement requires a healthy dose of bravery.

However, if guilt and shame are common themes for you, return to one of this programme's largest themes: **Quantum Tool #3**: **Align with Love or Above**, which is the idea that it's imperative to sit in the fire of your feelings, transmute them with love and quantum leap into the loftier "hi, vibes" range – see Tool #3.

Next, examine how you can boost your numbers in the upper levels of the Hertz Vibration Scale. Do you need to weave more self-care routines into your daily routine to feel love and above? Are there any practices in your personal cache that might bolster feelings of peace – prayer, perhaps, or spending additional time in nature? Can you look at something you've been unwilling to accept – for example, the loss of a friend or the dissolution of a relationship – and remind yourself that it's time to let go because so much wonder and bliss awaits ahead? I'm sure you see my point that it's always possible to shift your energy to higher vibes simply by tweaking your mindset.

Now let's assess where you stand in the chief domains of your life. Rate yourself between 1 and 5 in each of the areas listed overleaf: 1, meaning you don't feel very satisfied; 5, meaning you are off-the-charts elated with where you are. Please do not fall into judgement when evaluating; instead, approach each item with candour and compassion. This is, after all, merely feedback to help draw up your individual blueprint for positive change and guide you to the life of your dreams. (Feel free to add in any other life category you want to focus on.)

- Career
- Romance and love
- Friendships
- Family
- Self-love
- Health
- Finances, including savings, investments and assets
- Joyful activities and adventures
- Creativity
- Spirituality

Struggling to arrive at a number? Often, you can find where you fall in each category by thinking about what has shown up in your life recently, in your external reality. Each sphere of your life might carry a different vibe – and not only is that perfectly fine but it's also natural.

Let me share an example. I had a client named Jessica – an energy healer and coach – who was consistently challenged by magnetizing money but brilliant at attracting love. Jessica didn't need to focus on turning up her vibe in the area of romance, as her husband and the fun and adoration she found with him was enviable, but she *did* need to get real with what was happening in the realm of her career and personal finances. By engaging with the exercise that follows, she was able to create a new revenue stream that not only took her breath away (in a different kind of way than her man did) – she'd never seen her bank account so padded – but also fully aligned with her heart's mission of helping others.

Keep in mind that the first Quantum Tool, **Turn Up Your Vibrational Frequency**, isn't about mastering the vibe of exactly what you want in this moment, because sometimes when we try too hard to concentrate on what's missing, we can't align with it right away as it's too far out of our reach. Instead, the basic principle of Quantum Tool #1 is to figure out a way to feel better than you do about certain areas in this now moment. For Jessica, a multiple six-figure business initially felt like a monumental leap and therefore nearly implausible. And yet merely *thinking* about feeling abundant and receiving what she deserved for helping clients with her unique gifts felt nurturing. As such, we started small with that.

Now, take a look at every main area of your life where you rank on the lower side. Bust out that journal and write down three actionable items – or "manifesting lists" – that will assist you with increasing your "score." If you haven't dabbled in a creative endeavour for some time, start by writing down three things that would knock this number up some, whether it's taking a dance class, delighting your eyes on Pinterest or dusting off that guitar of yours that's been stashed in your broom closet.

Or, if you've neglected joyful activities and adventures (hello, pandemic and a crazy WFH schedule), concoct an exciting wish list that you can complete within a month's time, such as hitting up Happy Hour with friends who make you smile, seeing a live band and taking a weekend off to hike at the nearest national park.

NOTE: If at any time throughout this process, you encounter dark, recurring triggers that make you feel depressed or anxious in a way you can't shake, please reach out to a doctor or qualified therapist or coach. Some of the layers you discover within yourself may be difficult to face, and receiving support can nourish and protect you while *also* uplifting your vibes.

Turn Up Your Vibration with Breath Work

Your breath is your superpower – and an awesome instrument for change. By focusing on your breath, you can easily and effectively shift, move and increase your energy. In fact, the more connected you are to your breath, the more you'll be able to shift beyond what is, raise your energy and create a vibration aligned with all that you desire. You can also clear energy blocks and emotional energies that have been trapped in your body, thereby making room for – and encouraging – a higher frequency. What's more, breathing with awareness organically soothes your nervous system and this alone opens the mind, body and soul to greater thoughts, emotions and levels of consciousness.

Intentionally tapping into your breath creates a feeling of serenity and connectedness that will automatically turn up your vibration by creating a magnetic field within you. This allows you as a whole to *be* a higher vibration.

Breath work is a choice. It represents making up your mind to free yourself from any hindrances that are keeping you stuck and playing small.

EXERCISE

Breath Work

I recommend practising this exercise at least three times a week but daily for optimal benefit. (I, for one, perform this exercise daily, sometimes even twice when I'm particularly stressed.) You can continue doing it for as long as you feel that it helps you get centred and energized.

Sit up straight in a comfortable position, either cross-legged on the floor or in a chair with your feet planted on the ground. Start by becoming *aware* of your breath. Are you taking in pinched, shallow sips of air, or are you breathing deeply (expanding your belly), and smoothly? Again, no judgement here; just take note of what you discover. Why? Because we take roughly 20,000 breaths per day – and *how* we breathe can determine our physical, mental and psychological state.

Now, whatever pattern you've noticed, inhale and exhale naturally three times. On the fourth breath, inhale through your nose and simultaneously tighten the muscles in your pelvic floor and squeeze from your perineum front and back. (If you practise yoga, you know this as the Mula Bandha (Root Lock), which urges energy to ascend.) Grip these muscles for a few seconds, but don't strain yourself. Then, exhale naturally as you maintain the squeeze of your muscles throughout, if you can. Breathe in again as you maintain your squeezing or as you squeeze those muscles again, but this time also tighten the muscles up your spine toward your belly button. Keep the squeeze going as you aim to hold your breath for ten seconds. Try to take an extra sip of breath in while still holding your breath and sustain the squeeze from the base of your spine, through your pelvic region to your belly button and up your spine. Maintain that contraction of your muscles while holding your breath to the count of ten but, again, don't force it. Holding your breath should feel calm and powerful, not tense or exhausting.

Exhale through your mouth and take three normal long deep breaths in and out. Now, repeat the technique, but this time as you're breathing in and squeezing your lower core muscles, visualize a free-flowing stream of golden light moving up your spine from your tailbone to the back of your neck and then to the top, or crown, of your head. As the light reaches the top of your head, take in that extra sip of air and tighten your muscles even more toward your naval. Uphold that tightening as you hold your breath for ten seconds, continue to tighten your muscles even more, and visualize more light rising through your body and into your brain. Feel your energy open and expand with each passing second. Once you've counted to ten, slowly exhale through your mouth. Take three slow normal breaths and repeat this process.

Why is this recommended? Because as your energy moves from the base of your spine into your brain, it creates heightened awareness and can even generate euphoria.

As you may find, this is a powerful way to turn up your vibration! This breath work will take you out of living in survival mode – those three F's we discussed earlier (see page 80) – and away from blindly reacting to the circumstances around you. It'll keep you living in connectivity and vibing with joy and peace.

This exercise will help you feel better overall, and it'll also help you align your energy with your desires. The more you practise this breath work, the more you're conditioning your body to turn your frequency way, way up. And if you don't feel a sense of enriched awareness or higher energy right away, that's okay – just remember the struggles I encountered when I first started meditating. Keep trying and you'll see that, like anything else, the more you practise, the better you'll feel, and the more your energy – your vibe – will rise.

Week 2

Quantum Tool #2:
Connecting to the Quantum Field

When people learn that the quantum field exists, their consciousness instinctively opens. I've seen this happen hundreds of times. I mean, doesn't just *knowing* that there's an energetic field filled with unlimited possibilities, an ever-expanding and exciting button house, inspire you? And doesn't recognizing that you have the ability to connect to it and draw from it to turn your dreams into reality make you want to tap in and say *yes, yes, yes*, right this very second?

This Quantum Tool will help you get out of your logical mind and into your heart, which will lead you to the fresh, exciting and unlimited possibilities within the quantum field.

These exercises are designed to command your subconscious mind to align with the desires of your conscious mind. This coherence will open a gateway for you to connect with boundless energy and create new results in your life. We expand both our conscious and subconscious minds when we connect to our heart and something – an energy, a power, a truth – that is bigger than we are.

To quote Dr Joe Dispenza, "When you tap into the quantum field, you suspend thought. When you suspend thought, you raise your vibration. When you raise your vibration, you change your point of attraction, which changes your experiences and in turn changes your beliefs." Your "point" of attraction is the vibes you're sending out, which in turn attracts the energy for which you are a vibrational, or energetic, match.

The exercise opposite, Expand Your Awareness, is what vaulted me into working with energy. It opened my heart in an entirely new way and put me in touch with that vast eternal place we all come from. It was a game changer for dozens of my clients as well, but especially Andy.

Andy was feeling stuck and restless in his 9 to 5 job in the tech industry. He had done everything that was expected of him, and then some. He loved his job and the people with whom he worked and, although he was successful, he was eager to climb the corporate ladder and realize his full potential. Unfortunately, his colleagues received promotions and raises while he stayed exactly where he was – trapped.

Once Andy got out of his head and connected to the energy of who he was before he was born, he instantly became more magnetic. He tapped into the energy that had been there all along, which he simply wasn't able to see and feel until he *experienced* it.

The space you were in before you were born holds the reason you came here. It is where you were given your mission, your purpose, your essence or, as the spiritual teacher Caroline Myss calls it, your "sacred contract." When you journey to that place, its unlimited possibilities for becoming who you genuinely are start to feel real, tangible and feasible. You can feel these possibilities embedded in your energy field, which is what will then help your dreams become a reality.

Andy discovered a feeling of utter elation when he did this, and this connection shifted everything, from his mind and body to his heart and soul. He was able to send a signal of worthiness out to the universe instead of one of insecurity and inadequateness. This feeling translated into the vibe he brought with him to his job and within a month he received the promotion he had been longing for and working toward. Andy had this fantastic breakthrough because this exercise gave him the road map to connect to the quantum field and his own wisdom in a new way. It helped him see just how powerful his energy and thoughts truly are.

Expand Your Awareness

Do you remember who you were before you were born? Think about this: *You are more than a body.* Can you *feel* the truth of these words? If you can, where or how is that feeling hitting you? Does it give you the chills or make you smile or make you feel light and expansive or full of hope and awe? If you don't yet feel anything, stick with me and try the brief meditation and exercise that follows. Your subconscious is immensely powerful, and when you tap into it from a heart level, you'll remember things you may not have fully or consciously recollected until now.

When you can embody the wholeness that you feel by journeying back to who you were before you were born, you automatically turn up your vibration. Let's do this together now.

Before we dive in: have fun with this and do what feels good to you. You can record the questions opposite as a voice note for yourself if you prefer to listen to them. Also, be sure to have your journal and a pen ready (or one of your devices open) so you can free-flow write from this new, connected state and jot down any images, thoughts, guidance or feelings that surface during the meditation.

HEALING MEDITATION

Remember Who You Are

Optional recommended essential oil: Blend of blue tansy, blue chamomile, spruce leaf, frankincense and coconut.

This beautiful blend helps you feel grounded and safe as you begin to open your heart and expand your energy.

Long used by Native Americans for health and spiritual practices, it's a wonderful way to bring harmony into your life. (I use the doTERRA version of this blend, but you can use any version, or substitute some of the dominant oils it contains, such as frankincense and coconut.) If using the essential oil, place one drop of the blend on the bottom of your feet before performing this meditation. The large pores and energetic meridians there quickly absorb the oil and stimulate its therapeutic benefits.

Do this exercise one to three times throughout the week.

Set a timer for five minutes or choose an instrumental tune (one without lyrics) to listen to that lasts about that long. Sit up straight in a comfortable chair or, if it's restful for you, sit cross-legged on the floor. Place your hands on your heart and take in a deep breath. Ask yourself these five questions a few times to help you move out of your head and drop into your heart:

- *What was I doing before I was born?*
- *Where was I?*
- *How did it feel?*
- *What was I connected to?*
- *What images do I see in this realm?*

Don't think too much about what you're asking. Park your logical mind for a moment, let go and allow your soul to take you to your answers. Open your mind to whatever thoughts, pictures or ideas materialize.

Keep asking yourself these five questions.

Now, take long and slow deep breaths, in and out. Take three breaths for each question. For this part, five to ten minutes should give you enough time to dive into all the prompts. Then take another deep breath, slowly exhale, come back to the present and slowly open your eyes. Notice how content and connected you feel. While you're still in this state, write down what came through for you during this process.

Trust that whatever came up is perfect. If you went deep right away, take a minute to appreciate that and go to the next paragraph. If you didn't go as far as you would like at first, please stay with it and commit to trying again later in the day or first thing tomorrow morning. I promise that if you sit in stillness with the intention to connect to your higher self 1 to 3 times a week for a month, you will feel it eventually – and feel marvellous at that.

A few things to ask yourself: when you were breathing, could you feel a pure grace and sense of wholeness? Did you envision yourself feeling a part of something bigger? Did your worries dissipate with this feeling, even a little bit, even for a little while? Did you feel an expansion of energy in your heart?

When you connect to who you are on this level, you receive a profound reminder that you are, in fact, more than just a body. You begin to create access to the path of miracles, which will unfold right before your very eyes, every, single, day!

This brings me to another amazing success story I want to share, which occurred with my client, Brian. He found me a few weeks after life as we knew it got axed because of the pandemic. The dense energy of the fearful world, coupled with an enormous dip in his self-confidence and sense of self-worth, had shot him to an all-time low. He had created a career that was in line with his purpose and mission and had reached a great level of success in his business. His personal life, however, was in shambles. He felt imprisoned in his marriage and while he had been working on evolving personally and improving his relationship, he had to admit that he and his wife had grown continents apart.

Part of this was due to the fact that Brian lacked the ability to stand in his authentic power when his wife was around. Rather, he would shrink in her presence and drift around in the lower depths on the Hertz Vibration Scale. The last straw? She undermined him when he took the time to practise self-care in solitude, whether it was going for a run, meditating or doing yoga, all of which she deemed a "waste of time."

While I worked with Brian using all of the tools that I have shared with you here, this next one – the Crystalline Cylinder Connection – was particularly potent for him. It helped him pull back the energy he was losing to his wife's negativity and to own his confidence in a fresh, meaningful way. Harnessing this inner vibration and frequency allowed him to amicably separate from her. Once he was on his own and in a new space that naturally cultivated higher vibes, he began to feel optimistic and excited about the next chapter of his life. He was now in a place where he felt free to develop the businesses he truly wanted to construct, which his wife had not believed in nor thought he was capable of building. He was also free to deepen his spiritual practice as he had been striving to do for years. Brian used and still uses the Crystalline Cylinder Connection exercise any time he feels he is giving his power away to another person or circumstance.

The Crystalline Cylinder Connection exercise was shown to me in one of my own meditations. It's tremendously powerful – so much so it goes down as one of the most effective exercises for raising your vibes. Use it anytime you notice yourself leaking your energy or giving your power away say, by comparing yourself to others, caring what others think, focusing on what's not working or listening to the "haters." You can tap into this whenever you're running late and frustrated by a red light in traffic, or when your co-worker has yet again put the blame on you or when your partner left the dishes on the table for the third night in a row, or when you're worried and stressed about, well, *anything*.

It doesn't matter what triggered your annoyance or concern; what matters is that you take your power back right away and give your energy to the place where you can start to create miracles and magic: the quantum field. You can also do this anytime to magnify your vibe, turn up your energetic frequency and unite with the infinitely miraculous quantum field. The Crystalline Cylinder Connection exercise will transmute lower-level thoughts and heavier energies you might have inadvertently taken on. In our overdose of news binges during and post-pandemic, many of us have assumed weighty, low-vibe energies that are not serving us. This exercise was conceived to change that.

MEDITATION

The Crystalline Cylinder Connection

Optional recommended essential oil: *Lemon balm (also sometimes called Melissa). Lemon balm is a sweet, herbaceous and citrusy oil that operates as a natural tension fighter. It promotes feelings of calm and relaxation – the perfect state to be in to connect to and nurture higher vibrational energies.*

I recommend you do this exercise daily, throughout the week.

Begin this meditation with the intention to release any fear or negative, lower-level vibrations you may be latching onto and connect to the purest and most powerful light and energy available. Intentions are very different from expectations. They're like magnets that you set inside your energetic field. Set the intention to gain access to the energy source of love and infinite possibilities.

If you are using the essential oil, place one drop on your chest, where the centre of your heart and your *anahata* chakra are located. Straighten your spine in a sitting position, take a deep breath, hold it for three seconds and exhale through your mouth.

Next, return your breathing to normal, close your eyes and visualize a beautiful golden star inside your heart. Tune in to the freedom, light and grace inside this star. Acknowledge that these feelings already live inside your heart and that you have everything you could ever need right inside you, in this moment and always.

Notice as your fear and tension begin to fade in the rich golden glow of the star. Visualize a thin golden string moving up your body and out of the crown of your head. Watch this string move with ease; you don't need to do anything other than look on as it moves with your intention. Witness this golden light going up into the heavens and connecting to a star above your head. Feel the light, which is one with the star in your heart, expanding and yourself receiving even more love, connectedness, peace and contentment.

Now, focus your energy back on the star in your heart and watch as the same golden string moves down your torso and out of your feet, forming roots. These roots extend into the ground to anchor you. Note how supportive they feel, how grounding and safe. Notice as these roots go all the way down through the Earth's layers, down, down, down until they fasten onto a magnificent golden star in the crystalline core in the centre of the Earth.

Take a deep breath and feel the power of the connection you made. Breathe in the support, wisdom and safety that is there for you – again, in this moment and always. Now, start to stream this love that you are connected to from the planet into your heart, then from your heart and up to the heavens, from the divine source of love above you and back into your heart. As you stream this unconditional love, watch as the energy expands and the stream widens to become a crystalline cylinder that encompasses your entire being, protecting you and charging you with gorgeous, sparkling, high vibrations.

This high-vibrational crystalline energy circulates from one end of the cylinder through your body to the other. It feels amazing and alive and refreshing. It feels like home; like truth. Receive, receive, receive these feelings into every inch of your being. Let go of anything else you were giving your energy to as this crystalline energy fills you entirely. Pull back any energy you were leaking or giving away and focus on returning it back to this cylinder. Allow it to be cleansed and revitalized. Feel the love, the power, the purity, the infinite possibilities. Remember who you are, remember the love that *is* you. Receive and connect to the powerful, ever-knowing source of love that you are made of.

You can stay connected to this crystalline love cylinder as long as you need to. When you're ready to open your eyes, know that the energy you have generated will stay around you as you resume your day.

The more frequently you perform this exercise, the faster you can drop into this euphoric energy. This Crystalline Cylinder Connection exercise is a powerful starting point that will help you begin to connect to the quantum field with ease. If you do it every day, you will begin to build your energetic muscles with this powerful, quick and effective practice. You can also use it if you feel you have fallen off track and need a quick "pick-me-up" to help get you back on the right path again.

Week 3

Quantum Tool #3:
Align with Love or Above

This might be my favourite Quantum Tool of all. We were born to be innately loving beings, but somewhere along the way we may have lost sight of this fact and started fixating on things that don't really matter and don't support our life's purpose. When we bring it back to love – when we redirect our entire attention to love – we heal past traumas, change old stories and shift away from beliefs that harm us. By disconnecting from those old energy ties, we give the universe no choice but to deliver our dreams to us.

The energy of love is what bonds us as human beings. The more love you associate with a person, place or circumstance, the more you become energetically connected to it. Our emotions are the heart's sacred way of connecting to our minds and bodies. When we can get up close and personal with our emotions, we are able to dissolve the low vibrations inside us with love. This is especially powerful in a time of crisis.

In this Quantum Tool, **Align with Love or Above,** I take you in deep to begin to look at the beliefs that are in the way of vibing with the energy of love. A few common incorrect beliefs that many of us hold are: *I am not enough, I am not worthy of the life I desire,* and *I have to work hard to receive love.*

I will help you identify which beliefs you're carrying in both your conscious and subconscious minds that are not in alignment with love. I'll help you begin to create a powerful magnetic field that is connected directly to your soul and help you align with your mind and heart. This is the sweet spot of miracles!

EXERCISE

Open Your Heart

Optional recommended essential oil: Rose. The rose has long had a spiritual connection to higher powers and was associated with angels and heaven, even before its vibrations were measured. Translation? Rose oil has a very high vibration and will help you open and heal your heart chakra. This oil will also help you connect to self-love and compassion, as well as aid in eradicating old emotional wounds to make room for love.

If you are using rose essential oil (or spray), place the oil on your chest, in the centre of your heart. By doing this, you are setting the intention to consciously connect with the energy of love or above.

This meditation is the advanced, next level of the Crystalline Cylinder Connection exercise. As you have been practising the Crystalline Cylinder Connection exercise, you have been working on expanding your connection to the quantum field, where love reigns.

Your cells are now trained to tap in and connect quickly. Your energy and your heart are now ready to expand even more.

This is another exercise that will give you great benefits if you perform it daily.

Sit up straight, take a slow, deep breath in, and hold it for a count of five. Then, release your breath through your mouth. Repeat this twice more, taking note of each time you inhale and exhale. Feel how grounded you are but also lighter, freer and more connected to the expansive energy that surrounds you.

Now, return your breathing to normal and visualize a beautiful, golden cloud in the heavens. Notice how pure and vibrant this light feels. Tune in to the grace radiating from this light. See it reaching down to you from above and spilling directly into your heart.

See your name written on this peaceful, golden cloud. Watch it expand and become brighter and bigger. Now, see in your mind's eye another free-flowing stream of golden light falling from the cloud, down and into the crown of your head. With each breath you take, feel how the light dissolves any fears or doubts. They simply fade away with the river of light, out and into the ground, where they're instantly altered. Where they vanish.

Say this mantra out loud: "I am light. I am free. I am connected to love. I am powerful. I am love."

Continue to say this mantra as the golden light surges inside your head and down your throat to cushion your heart. Notice that this light revolves around and inside your heart-space like a lighthouse beam. Each time the light goes around, your energy grows more brilliant and expansive. Feel the fresh new vibrancy inside your heart.

Maybe you notice yourself smiling, maybe you are being shown some visions of what is to come, maybe you simply feel amazing. Relish this new-found energy and stay connected to it.

Allow the golden light to continue to permeate every cell and organ in your body. Visualize the high vibrational light travelling down each of your arms, into your hands and fingers, down your torso, inside the tissues lining your stomach and vital organs and down each of your legs into your feet.

Breathe into this serenity and grace. Allow it to continue to expand.

As this light starts to move through your tail bone and feet, feel yourself growing energetic roots. These roots go deep, deep, deep down, through the rocks and the roots and the soil, all the way down until they anchor into the beautiful, bright light at the centre of the Earth.

Feel the support of being connected to the heart of the Earth. Feel the planet's heart energy connecting to your roots and streaming green, healing energy up and back into your body.

Continue to breathe and focus on the mantra as you stream this golden light through your body and up into your golden cloud in the heavens. Imagine a crystalline cylinder of energy from the Earth to the heavens ensconcing your entire being. Feel into the security, love and glow you're emanating. Own it and *be* it.

You can perform this meditation once or repeat it twice – it's up to you. You can spend as much time as you need streaming the high vibrational energy up and down the crystalline cylinder you created. This meditation is not meant to be rushed; rather, savour every moment of it, much like love itself.

After doing this meditation, grab your journal and let your heart speak to you through your pen. Do not judge what comes through. Just allow your hand to move. Allow your words to flow and receive the nurturing words that appear.

Our hearts are always guiding us to the path of our highest fulfillment. And yet, most of us are too busy or distracted to stop, listen and connect to the true feelings of our hearts. The following exercise is extremely powerful and I recommend that you perform it daily this week and three to five times per week after that. You can also come back to it any time you feel triggered or disconnected.

EXERCISE

Connect with Your Heart

Optional Recommended Essential Oil: Chamomile. Sometimes called true, English or Roman chamomile, this herb has been dubbed the "plant's physician" because of its nourishing effects on other flora. Once used for courage during war by the Romans, it's one of the most effective essential oils for fostering tranquillity.

Collect your journal and pen and set them next to you. Light a candle and place a drop of chamomile essential oil on the insides of your wrists. Set the intention to release any feelings or emotions that are in the way of connecting with your heart. Sit up straight and take three long, slow, deep breaths.

Ask your heart the following questions, allow your thoughts to flow, but don't stop to write down your answers quite yet. Just ask your heart each of the questions, taking a minute or so to feel its replies:

- *What do you want me to know?*
- *What are you ready to let go of?*
- *What feeling do you have that needs to be seen?*
- *What are you craving in this moment?*
- *Why are you craving this?*
- *What are you committed to starting now?*
- *What does our higher power want me to know about you, my heart?*
- *What does my heart need in this moment?*

Go through these questions once again. This time, however, write down the answers that occur to you. After each answer, ask yourself, "Why am I feeling this way?" This will help you gain a greater understanding of what is happening. In understanding, accepting and acknowledging what is in your heart, you will begin to burst through the resistance you were holding that was blocking the frequency and feeling of love.

Each time you slow down, connect to your heart and let your inner energy speak, you're aligning your energy with love or above. You simply need to connect.

Week 4

Quantum Tool #4:
Reprogram and Rewire Your Mind

Now that you know how to gradually turn up your vibration, connect with the quantum field and make your heart your priority, it's time to go deeper. For best results do these exercises two or three times in the week.

We're all running a program, a story, a loop. This narrative courses in our minds whether we're aware of it or not. We receive programming in so many different ways: from childhood, from how we have learned to deal with trauma, loss, and/or disappointment and from what we allow into our space through the words of others, society, the media – you name it.

Most of us are not cognizant of the story, program or loop that sprints through our minds, that makes it challenging to shift. And yet, we can't change what we won't acknowledge or see. (Remember what Wayne Dyer once said: "When you change the way you look at things, the things you look at change.") Once we see the pattern of our narratives, we can rewire or shift it.

My client, Stella, who is a sex therapist by trade, faced a host of fears and doubts when the pandemic hit. Between the growing number of cases, government mandates, increased unemployment and quarantine, she convinced herself that no one would hire her and that she would lose the clients she already had.

That is not the way I saw it at all. I could see that it was, in fact, a splendid opportunity for her to attract new clients. I knew that many couples would need her services now more than ever, as issues they'd put on the back burner were emerging in the light, tension and closeness of quarantine and desperation.

Stella and I did a deep dive using this Quantum Tool, **Reprogram and Rewire Your Mind**. She shifted her story almost immediately. A week later, she reported she was getting an astonishing response from the universe and had already booked three new clients. She also created a virtual programme to help couples weather the crisis and was thrilled to begin marketing it.

The point is this: intentionally diving deep into our hearts and minds is a fresh and fabulous chance to rewire and reprogramme our thoughts, behaviours and, importantly, our energetic frequency.

First, I invite you to take an inventory of where you spend your time and energy.

• What are you allowing into your energy field?

- Are you listening to toxic news, unkind gossip or chronic, unconstructive criticism?
- Are you surrounding yourself with people and books and conversations that inspire and excite you? Or is it the converse?
- Is your living space a sanctuary or does it leave you feeling dispirited?

Start to notice as you go through the day where you're giving your energy and what you're letting through the gates to your heart and soul.

As we discussed, our subconscious mind is the Executive Director of the show of your life – the *real* showtime – 90 per cent of the time. And don't you want that 90 per cent to be attuned to precisely what you desire?

EXERCISE

Align Your Conscious and Subconscious Minds

One of the most powerful methods of aligning your subconscious and conscious minds is to ask questions that are in harmony with your vision, dreams and desires. In turn, your subconscious mind – with its own Google-esque algorithms – will search for the most fitting answer.

With this in, well, *mind*, ask yourself the following:

- *How can I allow more abundance to flow to me with ease and grace?*
- *What are the opportunities in my life I am not seeing?*
- *How can I allow more of that love energy to flow into my life and body?*
- *How is this situation/person/circumstance working out in my favour? What is it that it or they are trying to teach me?*
- *What are a few things that I could do, starting now, to attract my dreams and nail my vision?*
- *What are my next steps?*

Now create five questions of your own in your journal.

Practise consciously asking yourself some of these questions on a regular basis, particularly when you're triggered, and begin to watch how your behaviour shifts.

To take it up a notch, you can pick three to five of the questions to journal on every day. Get excited and ready for breakthroughs!

(Bonus: For an 18-minute audio meditation on rewiring and reprogramming your mind while you sleep, visit: www.suzanneadamsinc.com/sleep.)

This exercise will help you learn how to actually *converse* with your subconscious mind – like, have a full-on conversation with it. As we've discussed, your subconscious mind is constantly pursuing answers based on the specific questions that arise in your internal loop.

You more than likely have a pressing question to which you're always looking for an answer. For me, the magic question has long been, "How can I make this work?" This has served me well in my career, but it was futile when it came to my love life, where I should have been asking, "How can I open my heart more and focus on my true desires?" instead of pushing past my intuition and trying to force things to work.

Week 5

Quantum Tool #5:
Repurpose Your Energy

Even if we're on a clear, committed path to growth and healing, we're inescapably going to find ourselves triggered.

As you have learned, I consider triggers not to be weapons of massive personal destruction – as they were in the past for me – but as opportunities for motivation, change and a higher vibrational frequency. After all, triggers exist to reveal what we need to look at in our lives and within ourselves to be a bright, robust and unflinching energetic match to all that we want to beckon into our world.

The energy of anger lights a fire that can galvanize you and exact terrific change, much like the energy of envy. Meanwhile, the energy of melancholy can result in heightened creativity. If you take the emotional momentum that's felt in those inevitable, low, "bye" vibes, you not only raise your vibrational frequency but actually accomplish something with the unpleasant feelings that have been evoked. This means you can draw in what you desire faster than you could *without* the trigger. Just think of how many mind-blowing, awe-inspiring songs, novels, films, paintings – even business moves! – that were created from a place of rage or heartache or jealousy or regret!

Indeed, one of the biggest mindset shifts you have at your disposal is viewing your triggers with gratitude. Absolute gratitude. A synonym for "to trigger" is "to incite" and to be able to be lit on fire and moved not into numbing yourself but into dynamic, beneficial action. Now that's a *gift*, so much so that you want to work this tool to the point that you actually *thank* the person, issue or situation that provoked you. After all, it captured your attention and upped your frequency on the Hertz Vibration Scale. Tuning in to the exercises in this section will repurpose this energy into gold.

Heal Through Your Pain
(You Heard Me Right)

As discussed in Tool #5, triggers are a tremendous chance for healing and an awesome catalyst for change. Yes, they're uncomfortable – and that may be too mild of a way to put it. Rather, they downright *stink*. And yet, within them lies an outrageously potent opportunity. If you can move through your triggers mindfully, the very things that needle you can also help you release what's kept you from freedom, joy and peace. And once you let go? You'll have the space for your creative energy to flow and for your dreams to manifest.

When you're triggered, which may show up as feeling aggravated, shocked, disgusted, on the verge of tears or straight-up angry, follow this process and watch the experience change as you turn up your vibration.

EXERCISE

Shift Your Triggers into Gold

Start by noticing the trigger, by *recognizing* that you're triggered in the first place. This takes calm, conscious breathing and perspective, sure, but once you start practising the technique of being curious about your emotional responses, you'll find that it'll be easier to do (if not automatic), and that you, in turn, will be less reactive.

Then, ask yourself this:

- *What is this really about? Is this about me or the person triggering me?* (Hint: It's always about you, but let your soul tell you that.)
- *What is this bringing to the surface?*
- *What is it suggesting I change my viewpoint on or release (this could be a story, a belief, a memory, a behaviour, a thought pattern or a relationship)?*

- *What is the trigger, exactly?* (Here's an example from my personal archives: My boyfriend pulls away or needs a little bit of space. While it is perfectly normal that this can happen, even if it's only for a day or two I feel triggered to a boiling point. Instead of lashing out at him with my wounded feelings, I take the opportunity to go within and use this time to do profound healing on myself.)

- *What is the story here?*
- *Where did the emotional wound originate?*
- *What do I need for healing looking forward and not backward?*

Once you've answered these questions – again, there are no right or wrong replies, and you shouldn't constrain yourself in any way – close your eyes and visualize your soul telling you that it's now a different time. That you're at a wiser age and have undergone transformational experiences. That you no longer need the protection your subconscious mind cultivated when the original hurt took place.

To get back to my own trigger with my boyfriend … I thought about it, and then thought about it some more. The whole trigger stemmed from high school. I had a boyfriend then who adored and cherished me, but I didn't always treat him very well. In turn, after we broke up I thought he would still be around patiently waiting to get back with me. Unbeknown to me, he started dating one of my best friends. The story I began to tell myself and the meaning I gave it was this: no one I love chooses me. No one *fights* for me. The story became super-ingrained in my cells. Layers upon layers were added over the years, so much so that I could have sworn my DNA went through some revisions. The ongoing, interior narrative sounded something like, "I have to work hard and hide who I really am to get someone to love me." This wound was old and deep and not even true. It was a false meaning I had created and taken on. This trigger had nothing to do with my boyfriend and everything to do with me. It was in my best interest to give him space and do my own inner healing.

These were deep wounds and they hurt. So, I could sit with my aggrieved child – this teenage version of me, and the adult she became – and let her, let *myself*, feel all of this. I could also decide to stay the way I was or I could think of this from a higher perspective, where better vibes reside:

a) Was any of this true? No, actually. I knew and acknowledge I am a loving, generous, high-vibing woman who is worthy of a love story that will take my breath away.
b) Would God *really* send me into this world to never experience a profound, romantic, soul-connection kind of love? Of *course* not.

c) Is there potential in the quantum field for this to heal instantly? Oh my goodness, *yes.* (This question alone will change your life, if you let it!)

Which brought me to my next question:

d) Is there a place in the quantum field where my man is solid and sure and wants to rock my world and be my rock at the same time? Yes, again!

Now I know what is really true and that I have options (we always have options – actually an abundance of options – and tuning in to the truth will always provide healing and detachment). It is this: I can heal the wounds that created these triggers and focus on the potential that I want, not on the memories of the past.

You can do the same with this healing meditation.

MEDITATION

Heal Your Inner Child

Optional recommended essential oil: Peppermint. Peppermint is a great way to cleanse your palate – and I don't just mean that literally. It aids in clearing your energetic field of past hurts that have led to triggers in the present.

If you're using this essential oil, place one drop of peppermint on the inner arch of each of your feet. Peppermint is effective for moving and releasing energy and, again, the large pores and energetic meridians in your feet quickly absorb the oil and disperse therapeutic benefits.

Do this meditation two to three times through the week as you will uncover new layers each time you perform this.

Close your eyes. Imagine the sun or a beautiful, glowing light in the heavens among the clouds. Connect to the golden light's serene vibrations. (This connection should feel easy and familiar after practising the preceding meditations. If you're having trouble with it, please go back to the other meditations for a tune-up!)

Call in your higher self, angels, God, universal consciousness – whatever vibes with you. Ask to be shown any and all of the wounds related to this trigger and obstacle in the way of making a quantum leap and attracting the glorious, real result you have aligned with in the quantum field.

(Note: You don't need to go searching for old, buried wounds and live in them. Let your subconscious and your higher power show you what needs to be seen. Sometimes we can quantum leap in healing by tapping into the frequency of a trigger and looking into the future and not so much into the past. Allow yourself to be shown all that is necessary, by a power that is greater and wiser than you. See the unlimited possibilities that you brought to the forefront of your awareness. As you're shown the wounds that emerge, take note of the age you were when they happened. And if only one wound appears, then trust that.)

Invite your inner child to sit with you as you go through these wounds. See them at every age you experienced these hurts. See them at age three, when they didn't feel safe to be authentically *them*. See them at age seven, not feeling worthy of the wishes that were just beginning to cement in their mind. See them at age sixteen, broken-hearted and creating damaging beliefs not aligned with romantic love. See them in college and beyond, searching for connection.

In your mind's eye, see your inner child at all these different ages standing in a line. Visualize yourself in the present day and time. Invite each version of your inner child to come forward, one at a time. (There is no rush here, so take as long as you need while going through this process.)

Embrace them and tell them how perfect, whole and loved they are. Ask them what they want to tell you. Ask them what they want from you now, as an adult with experience and wisdom. Listen. Watch a light arrive from heaven and journey into their heart and then travel to your heart, back to their heart and to your heart again, backward and forward. Continue this until you see both of your broken hearts become whole.

Once the three-year-old version of you has a whole heart, watch them merge with the present-day you and grow roots. Recreate your new reality with a whole, healthy version of you, one who is grounding roots in the new time and space and reality you have built to align with your vision in the quantum field.

Repeat this with every wounded version of yourself; each inner child who was revealed. If any new ones pop up during meditation, go through the process with them as well. At the end of each process, repeat the following: "It is safe to be loved. It is safe to give and receive love. I am whole. I am perfect. I am love."

After each healed version of your inner child merges, visualize them in front of you in the present day. Picture both of you with healed and whole hearts, ready to feel safe, ready to realize your big, bold dreams. Visualize both versions of yourself experiencing the world from a higher level of consciousness. Watch the heart healing between you and them and integrate this new vision and declaration into your current reality.

To help integrate this healed self, you can use the mantra, *"I am healed, I am whole. Everything I desire flows to me with grace and ease. My desires are mine because they are my birthright. Divine sacred union, love, abundance, joy – or whatever I want – is mine, because it just is. It is my destiny in this moment and forever after."*

Whether you're feeling light and free, or are still releasing emotions after this meditation, grab your journal or the notes section on your device and ask your inner child if there's anything else they need to tell you to further assimilate your healing. It may be words of gratitude, praise or simply another emotion that is longing to be felt and freed. There is no right or wrong here, just presence and healing.

Tears will likely come up in this meditation. If they do, let them flow. Tears are a release and a reprogramming, and they'll ultimately help you turn up your vibration. If you don't cry, that's okay too. Remember that there are layers and layers within you, and everyone's process is unique.

Repeat this meditation as often as you need to when triggers arise. Be kind to yourself and give yourself extra love and nurturing on the days you go through this process.

Remember, you are loved.

(News flash: A side effect of doing this exercise is that your trigger will dissipate and new possibilities and dreams will show up immediately!)

EXERCISE

Accentuate the Positive

Do this exercise twice during the week and afterwards revisit it anytime something upsetting or irritating is happening.

There is always a silver lining and a path to freedom when we're triggered. This exercise helped me land virtual teaching opportunities with Fortune 500 companies in the middle of the pandemic, as well as help countless clients create new revenue streams inside their businesses, mend or end relationships, and strengthen their self-confidence.

When something feels like a setback or a failure, or when something negative is happening to you, it's really important to shift your mindset around the situation. Looking for ways in which the current, less-than-ideal situation could actually be working on your behalf can change everything.

Use the questions below to turn up your frequency and reprogram your cellular structure and neural pathways by tuning in to how the situation is working on your behalf:

- *How is this working out for me?*
- *How is this working toward my best intentions?*
- *What is this showing me to let go of?*
- *What do I need to see here that I am missing?*
- *How can I repurpose this energy to align with my highest desires?*
- *What potential do I desire to intentionally align with in the quantum field instead of this?*

Write your answers down. Study them. *Feel* them. Then, repeat this set of questions anytime you're triggered. You'll find manifesting power with this process and will start realizing your dreams.

Week 6

Quantum Tool #6:
Activate Your Vision *in the NOW*

Things are getting juicy now! You have elevated your consciousness and heart to new heights. You have let go and are tapping into an energy and vibration that is going to blow your mind. Quantum Tool #6 **Activate Your Vision *in the NOW*** is about taking it all to the next level.

As human beings, we can often get stuck on what *is*, instead of what we desire. If our energy and focus is too hung up on what is, we can never reach where we want to go because we can barely imagine it, let alone *feel* it. But every process and exercise we have completed up until this point has allowed us to receive in a whole new way.

I once had a client named Sarah, who is one of the sweetest souls I've ever met. She is a mom of seven (yep, I said seven) and when she first came to work with me, she felt terribly deflated, as if she could never have a life of her own while tending to all of her children. I could see how bright this woman's light really was, even in the dimmed-down state it was in when we first met. She went deep on each of these tools and her dedication to reclaiming her light and energy was beyond impressive.

I won't say that it was one and done for her, as it usually isn't. She kept showing up. She continued to return to the exercises until they became imprinted in her mind and body. In time, she was able to create a life that was finally on her terms while also allowing her to take care of her family. Tuning into the energy of what she desired instead of the never-ending carpool lines and her four daily loads of laundry was a game changer for her on many levels.

She was able to energetically create her vision and vibe with it as though nothing else existed, even though her reality was far from what her vision held. One day at a time, she began to have breakthroughs. Neighbours and members of her community showed up out of the woodwork to help her. She began to create space and time for her own meditation practice, as well as for travelling and business development. She healed her heart and quadrupled her monthly income in her network marketing business after a few short months. Inspiring, isn't it?

EXERCISE

Manifest Magic

When it comes to manifesting, your BIG WHY is a powerful magnet that will help draw your manifestations toward you. I recommend you do this three times a week.

Many people don't even know what they are playing for or why. Let's take some time today to dream big and create clarity and intention around where we are going and WHY we want to go there!

Read this out loud:

"The reason my dreams are important is because I am a worthy human being and when I am happy, the world is a better place. When I am aligned and in service, others automatically follow suit and the world begins shifting in a powerful way.

"My dreams will change the world for good! The more open my heart is, the faster my dreams will flow to me. The more abundant I am, the more I can do further good and create joy on this planet."

Now, give yourself permission to truly dream BIG by taking out that journal again and answering the following:

- *If I had ten million dollars flow into my bank account today, I would …*
- *If money were no object and I could do anything I wanted, I would …*
- *I am my happiest when I am …*
- *I am most of service to others when …*
- *I am committed to creating my dreams because …*

Focus on the feelings you have created while letting yourself imagine these possibilities – which, to remind you, are yours for the taking. Honour the commitment you made to show up for these dreams.

Now: what are three action steps you can take today in the direction of these big dreams? (If your action steps are the same each time, that's okay.) List them in your journal.

At this point, you not only want to connect to the quantum field, but also to *draw* it to you. To do this, you will increase your vibration based on your vision of the future. You will take the space that you have internally created through the healings and clearings of each preceding Quantum Tool and fill that in energetically with your vision and the energy to match it.

(Bonus: To access an audio meditation to magnetize your desires to you from the quantum field, go to: www.suzanneadamsinc.com/magnetize.)

This is probably the most liberating Quantum Tool of all because it functions as a commitment to no longer allowing your past traumas, stories and programming to dictate your present or future. You will be able to catapult yourself into a new reality with every cell of your being, as well as utilize the real-world tools you have learned throughout this programme.

You can also do any of the other meditations you have learned under the previous Quantum Tools that worked well for you instead if you prefer.

Staying in the Quantum Flow

Quantum Tool #7:
Follow the Flow of Synchronicity and Divine Guidance

This is the exciting part where you start to notice the signs and synchronicities; now you have an entire arsenal of tools and exercises to come back to as different life experiences show up!

In Tool 6, **Activate Your Vision *in the NOW*,** I told you the improbable story of the woodpecker that led me to move across the country to sunset dreams and ocean views. That was only one of many success stories that came through the flow of synchronicity and divine guidance.

I had a client named Jen who proved the magic of this Quantum Tool and blew all of our minds, including those of her husband, friends and family. When she came to me, she was six months pregnant and restless. Once she learned about divine guidance and synchronicity, she chose to throw all logic out of the window and trust what she was being shown. She was sitting in meditation one day and doing the Quantum Tool visualizations when she kept hearing the word "move." At first, she was confused, but after hearing this repeatedly, she tuned into her heart and realized her deep longing for more space. She had three other children and they were bursting at the seams of the house in which she, her husband and the children lived.

In another meditation, she saw the ideal house for her family, from the slope of its roof to the colour of its paint. After hearing the word in meditation, she saw "MOVE" on a licence plate, and then "It's time to move" on a street sign beside her office that she had never noticed before. She realized she had to follow her heart; that she wanted to sell her house and buy a larger home before her next child was born, even if she wasn't sure she and her husband could pull it off.

Utilizing the power of divine guidance she connected with as part of this Quantum Tool, she was able not only to sell her home within seven days – without even listing it with a real estate agent – but also to receive an offer $5,000 (£3,750) over her asking price (this was well before getting offers over the listed price was a thing) and a backup offer in case the first one fell through. Talk about miracles and divine flow!

Then, she found the house she had seen in her meditation. It was perfect for her growing family, although well outside of the price range she and her husband had set for themselves. Realtors advised her to keep looking, as the owners of the home had not been willing to budge on any previous offers. She wouldn't listen. She continued to tap into her heart, inner guidance system and the quantum field. Her external events unfolded in line with her intentions.

She got the house in the price range they could afford and had the home ready to move into just as she went into labour. She left her old home to go to the hospital to deliver her baby and came home from the hospital with her fourth child into her new, perfectly manifested home that had been sent to her from the universe. That is the power of this process – and it's awesome.

We are all being guided by something that is so much bigger than we are – and the messages come in all different forms. Birds and animals are definitely some of the "messengers" that people have noticed and interpreted in different ways. Sometimes it's a "chance" encounter. Others hit your heart in a new way. Found objects or overheard bits of conversation or shop signs or unexpected detours can suddenly take on new, significant meaning and lead us down a path we would've otherwise never found in the forest of life.

The Quantum Tool process is completed with an act of surrender and trust. We each get to be guided. This is the tool that will keep you on track as you embark on your new journey of creating a life that'll blow your mind.

When we align our energy with what we desire and we are open and receptive, there is no way that our desires will not find their way to us. It is impossible. The path, however, is different for each of us.

This seventh Quantum Tool, **Follow the Flow of Synchronicity and Divine Guidance**, teaches you how to notice when the universe is trying to help you by catching your attention, showing you the way and lining everything up for you.

EXERCISE

Notice the Signposts

To hone in on this natural part of the relationship you have with the universe, start this process by opening your eyes – really, really opening your eyes. This begins not with the signs and synchronicities you'll find around you but within. Then ask yourself:

- *Where in my life would I like clarity and direction on something that's filled me with uncertainty?*
- *What "coincidences" have I stumbled upon lately that seem meaningful in a way I can't quite articulate (yet)?*
- *What songs, phrases, memes, road signs, licence plates – even tattoos – have I noticed lately that seemed to strike some unknown chord within me?*
- *What flora or fauna keep appearing in my life?*
- *Why are these things resonating with me?*
- *Which friends, acquaintances, family members or colleagues I haven't seen for some time have suddenly emerged in my life again? Why?*

> - *What knowledge do I think I have stored deep down that has flashed in my mind but I haven't given adequate attention to?*
>
> Answering these questions can be wonderfully revealing, just as they can be reflected back upon as directing you toward where you should ideally be heading (or, on the other hand, what, where and whom you should be dodging at all cost).

By now, you've seen the magic that signs and synchronicities have had in my life, as well as the lives of my clients. Now it's your turn to be wooed, wowed and moved by this ever-knowing, all-loving presence.

Jump in, savour this fresh new life that is waiting to be created. Understand that you are a limitless human being and this is truly only the beginning. Your dreams are planted in your heart for a reason and now is your time to go out and get them!

My Wish For You

It's Your Turn to Quantum Leap

You've now completed the exercises in the Workbook and have armed yourself with all the practical Quantum Tools to create the life you deserve and desire. But these tools aren't a one-and-done type of thing. Revisit them often and return to the Workbook frequently, as the more you practise these Quantum Tools, the more exciting they – and your life – will become.

Before I leave you, I want you to *really* understand this: you have a choice in every moment to move from average and ordinary to exceptional and extraordinary. You have everything you could ever desire right inside your heart, and within your energy and your soul. It's up to you to unlock it.

I created this programme, this book, this process, to help you understand how to use your energy to build a life that will set your soul on fire and maybe, just maybe, blow your own mind!

My wish for you is you get so good at using these tools that love or above becomes your middle name; that you manifest "unrealistic" miracles often; and that you radiate a vibe so high that you become the woman or man who lights up a room the moment you arrive, simply with your presence.

Thank you from the bottom of my heart for taking this journey with me. I am grateful for your time, your open heart, your energy and your presence. I am sending you so much love and magic – and infinite quantum vibes!

xoxo
Suzanne

Acknowledgments

I'd like to thank my family and friends who have supported me and cheered me on each step of the way. I'd like to offer a huge thank you to every single client that I have ever had the privilege and honor to support. Thank you to each company and individual that has hired me to share my process and knowledge with your audience. Thank you to my team for being a part of such a powerful mission.

Thank you to Welbeck Publishing for your support through this process.

And a final thanks to you, the reader. Without you none of this is even possible. I am sending each and every one of you more love and gratitude than you will ever know.

Further Resources

Zukav, G (1991), *The Seat of the Soul*, Rider Publishing
Hanson, R (2014), *Hardwiring Happiness*, Rider Publishing
Carpenter, H (2003), *The Genie Within*, CreateSpace Independent Publishing Platform
Dispenza, J (2019), *Becoming Supernatural*, Hay House
Hawkins, D (2020), *The Map of Consciousness Explained*, Hay House
Levine, P (1997), *Waking the Tiger*, North Atlantic Books
Dyer, W (2012), *Wishes Fulfilled*, Hay House

About Us

Welbeck Balance publishes books dedicated to changing lives. Our mission is to deliver life-enhancing books to help improve your wellbeing so that you can live your life with greater clarity and meaning, wherever you are on life's journey. Our Trigger books are specifically devoted to opening up conversations about mental health and wellbeing.

Welbeck Balance and Trigger are part of the Welbeck Publishing Group – a globally recognized independent publisher based in London. Welbeck are renowned for our innovative ideas, production values and developing long-lasting content. Our books have been translated into over 30 languages in more than 60 countries around the world.

If you love books, then join the club and sign up to our newsletter for exclusive offers, extracts, author interviews and more information.

www.welbeckpublishing.com   **www.triggerhub.org**

 welbeckpublish
 welbeckpublish
 welbeckuk

 Triggercalm
 Triggercalm
 Triggercalm

WELBECK
BALANCE

TRIGGER™
Your Specialist Mental Health & Wellbeing Hub

NOTES

NOTES

NOTES